Badminton

Badminton

Eighth Edition

Margaret Varner Bloss

Former World Badminton Champion

R. Stanton Hales

The College of Wooster

Boston   Burr Ridge, IL   Dubuque, IA   Madison, WI
New York   San Francisco   St. Louis
Bangkok   Bogotá   Caracas   Lisbon   London   Madrid   Mexico City
Milan   New Delhi   Seoul   Singapore   Sydney   Taipei   Toronto

796.345
BLO

McGraw-Hill Higher Education

*A Division of The **McGraw-Hill** Companies*

BADMINTON: WINNING EDGE SERIES, EIGHTH EDITION

Published by McGraw-Hill, an imprint of The McGraw-Hill Companies, Inc., 1221 Avenue of the Americas, New York, NY 10020. Copyright © 2001, 1994, 1990, 1987, 1980, 1975, 1971 by The McGraw-Hill Companies, Inc. All rights reserved. No part of this publication may be reproduced or distributed in any form or by any means, or stored in a database or retrieval system, without the prior written consent of The McGraw-Hill Companies, Inc., including, but not limited to, in any network or other electronic storage or transmission, or broadcast for distance learning.

Some ancillaries, including electronic and print components, may not be available to customers outside the United States.

This book is printed on acid-free paper.

1 2 3 4 5 6 7 8 9 0 QPF/QPF 0 9 8 7 6 5 4 3 2 1 0

ISBN 0-697-34534-3

Vice president and editor-in-chief: *Kevin T. Kane*
Executive editor: *Vicki Malinee*
Developmental editor: *Tricia R. Musel*
Senior marketing manager: *Pamela S. Cooper*
Associate media producer: *Judi David*
Project manager: *Joyce Watters*
Production supervisor: *Kara Kudronowicz*
Coordinator of freelance design: *David W. Hash*
Photography by: *Bill Leslie Photography*
Photo research coordinator: *John C. Leland*
Supplement coordinator: *Sandra M. Schnee*
Compositor: *Interactive Composition Corporation*
Typeface: *10/12 Palatino*
Printer: *Quebecor Printing Book Group/Fairfield, PA*

www.mhhe.com

PREFACE

▶ Whom is This Book For?

Badminton, the eighth edition, is designed for all players who wish to learn or improve their badminton game; information presented is suitable for and useful to players at all levels: backyard, school, club, and tournament. The book provides an organized description of how best to play and enjoy the game. Beginners can learn the essentials by following the step-by-step instructions in the text. Advanced players can refresh forgotten techniques by skimming the table of contents and paragraph headings to locate material.

▶ Features to This Edition

Badminton starts out by discussing the origins of the game and its special contributions. Every badminton player must learn not only *how* to execute fundamental techniques but also *when* and *why* they should be used. The instructions, analyses, drills, and self-evaluation questions in the book address these issues. Also included are sections on equipment and tournament play, a glossary, and an expanded reference section of the growing literature on badminton.

Enhancing the book are the precision of the line drawings and the realism of the photographs. The artist has made it possible for readers to learn the subtle muscle changes that occur in various arm and body movements.

Special features that further enhance *Badminton* include:

- Each chapter opens with a list of objectives and closes with a bulleted summary to reinforce the major points covered.
- Key terms are highlighted in boldface type in the text and defined in corresponding boxes. Both approaches facilitate the reader's comprehension of vocabulary.
- Assessments appear at the end of applicable chapters to assist the reader in reviewing skills and improving performance.

▶ Supplements

To facilitate the use of *Badminton* in the classroom, a printed Test Bank is available to instructors. The various types of questions allow for quick assessment of the basic rules, strategies, and principles of badminton.

▶ Acknowledgements

The authors would like to thank Dr. Paul Gustafson at Augusta State University for his insightful review of the seventh edition.

CONTENTS

CONTENTS

CHAPTER 1

BADMINTON
A SHORT HISTORY

OBJECTIVES

After reading this chapter, you should be able to do the following:

- Discuss the history of badminton.
- Understand how the modern Olympic sport of badminton developed from an ancient pastime.

KEY TERMS

While reading this chapter, you will become familiar with the following terms:

▶ **Battledore**

▶ **Serve**

▶ **Shuttlecock**

INTRODUCTION TO BADMINTON

". . . to play shuttlecock methinks is the game now . . ."
Two Maids of Moreclacke **(Anon), 1609**

Devotees of sports take pride in tracing the roots of their games as far back as possible. In this search, few sports can match badminton, for its roots are clearly established in civilizations that flourished over two thousand years ago, and its development is chronicled century by century to the present.

ANCIENT TIMES

The **shuttlecock,** badminton's unique object, was central to the ancient Chinese game of *Ti Jian Zi,* or shuttlecock kicking. Evidence of this game dates back at least to the first century B.C. Shuttlecock kicking was also popular in the neighboring areas of Japan, India, and Siam and soon found its way to Sumeria and Greece. Although the shuttle was usually hit by feet or hands, various bats were occasionally used as well.

Exactly how and why the shuttlecock's popularity became so widespread so early is not clear. It is reasonable to assume, however, that feathers from eaten fowl were plentiful and that perhaps methods of storing them, such as sticking them into cork or balls of yarn, led to the discovery of a delightful plaything. The fascination and enjoyment of striking a shuttlecock back and forth, either in gentle play or in fierce competition, is a thread running through the ages.

MEDIEVAL TIMES AND SEVENTEENTH CENTURY

English woodcut illustrations from the fourteenth and fifteenth centuries show peasants batting a shuttlecock to each other with rectangular wooden paddles, and by the late sixteenth century this had become a popular children's game. The word **"battledore,"** a derivative of the Old English word *batt,* was given to the striking instrument for cudgel. William Shakespeare makes reference to battledore and shuttlecock many times in his plays and other writings. Samuel Pepys in his *Diary* makes reference to "shittlecock."

The social status of battledore-shuttlecock rose in the seventeenth century, as it became a pastime for royalty and the leisured classes. As such, in France, it was called *jeu de volant,* or "game of shuttlecock." A 1638 etching from the French court shows a fine gentleman volleying a shuttle by himself with a well-strung battledore in each hand. The Parisian artist Jean Chardin painted a masterpiece "Jeune Fille Jouant au Volant" (Young Girl Playing at Shuttlecock), which now hangs in Florence's famous Uffizi Gallery.

Prince Henry, son of King James I of England, is said to have been "playing at shuttle-cocke with one farr taller than himself and hitting him by chance with the shuttle-cocke upon the forehead." This quotation from *Two Maids of Moreclacke* suggests that even as early as the 1600s there was an element of real competition in the game.

In Germany and Scandinavia the game became known as federball, or feather-ball, and in 1650 Queen Kristina of Sweden built a special court for herself and visiting noblemen near Stockholm's Royal Palace. Even Catherine the Great is said to have played in Russia.

At this patrician level, the shuttle was hit into play at the start of a rally by a servant, hence the term, "to **serve**."

EIGHTEENTH CENTURY

Battledore and shuttlecock was an accepted institution in Europe in the 1700s. The French author de Garsault devoted six paragraphs to the shuttlecock in a book on the *Art of the Tennis Racket Maker,* and he lamented the age-old problem that shuttles cost too much and were "quickly spoiled." Artwork also continued to record the game's popularity. In Poland, Adam Manyoki painted "Young Prince Sulkowski" with a shuttle and battledore, and an English portrait (c. 1740) of the young Earl of Dysart depicts him similarly.

The first evidence of battledore-shuttlecock in America dates to this period. The popularity of the game in England during King James's time certainly caused it to spread to the colonies, but exactly when is not known. Yet, in 1742, a London merchant wrote Mrs. Ross of Annapolis, "You sent for shuttlecocks and no battledores, whether you intended to omit them I could not guess, but as they are used together, I sent them so, with variety, I hope 'tis not wrong." A 1766 advertisement in New York by James Rivington stated that he sold battledores and shuttlecocks. A 1790 tapestry from colonial Williamsburg shows two boys hitting a shuttlecock back and forth on a Virginia hillside.

Throughout this time, the game appears to have been especially popular with young people, but the object of the game was still primarily to hit the shuttle *to*

▶ **Shuttlecock**
Official (and ancient) name for shuttle or "bird," badminton's unique projectile.

▶ **Battledore**
The instrument used to strike a shuttle-cock; a derivative of the Old English word batt, for cudgel.

▶ **Serve**
Stroke used to put the shuttle into play at the start of each rally.

each other, or to oneself, and to keep it in the air as long as possible. The idea of a net and of trying to prevent one's partner from returning the shuttle was still a century away.

NINETEENTH CENTURY

By the early 1800s, battledore and shuttlecock was a regular fixture in English country houses. These country gentlemen were sportsmen; and one in particular, the seventh Duke of Beaufort, issued a series of books on sports and games named after his Gloucestershire estate, Badminton House. His family, the Somersets, were avid players at shuttlecock: inscriptions on the vellum heads of their battledores record rallies consisting of 2,117 shots on January 12, 1830, and of 2,018 shots in February, 1845.

The transition from battledore-shuttlecock to badminton, building slowly for over eighteen hundred years, quickened in the 1850s and 1860s. One day, someone stretched a string across the middle of the Front Hall at Badminton House, making an elementary net. Whether it was the Somerset children, one of the Duke's sporting friends, or a visiting Army officer who had seen such a net in India, no one can be certain. In any case, the "new game" *badminton battledore* was advertised by a London toy dealer in 1860, and by 1867 a rather formal game, with lines and real nets, was being played in India by English officers and their families. Although the precise birthplace and birthdate of modern badminton is thus impossible to specify, it is certain that the latter took place before the March 1874 inauguration of modern lawn tennis.

From 1870 to 1900, badminton came of age as a competitive indoor sport. The first rules appeared in India in 1873, and clubs were formed throughout the British Isles to promote competition. The first tournaments were held there early in the 1890s, and the first All-England Championships were held in 1899. Until the 1920s, the major titles were contested by the English, Scots, and Irish. Rules varied until about 1905, when the Badminton Association of England adopted and promulgated uniform new rules that are, in essence, those followed today as the Laws of Badminton.

THE MODERN GAME: BADMINTON IN THE WORLD

Beginning in the 1920s, badminton spread first to northern Europe, becoming especially popular in the Scandinavian countries, and then to North America and the Far East. The Irishman who had dominated the All-Englands in the early 1920s, Frank Devlin, was instrumental in promoting the game in Canada, and the interest in badminton developed by the British in India and Malaya (later Malaysia) was soon found throughout Asia, as one country after another rose to the top ranks: Thailand and Indonesia in the 1950s, Japan in the 1960s, China in the 1970s, and Korea in the 1980s.

The International Badminton Federation was formed in 1934 with nine member countries and grew to more than eighty-five affiliated nations in the 1980s. Various international competitions for teams and individuals were instituted in the postwar years (see chapter 8) and by 1979 the game had become fully professional. Open tournaments throughout the world attracted the top players to a touring career similar to that of other professional athletes.

Badminton took a giant step when the International Olympic Committee voted in 1985 to add badminton to the Olympic program. Making its Olympic debut in 1992 as a full medal sport, badminton solidified its position as a recognized international sport, and it was among the first sports at the 1996 Atlanta Olympics to sell out its tickets. By 1999, the International Badminton Federation had grown to 138 member nations. Badminton offers a world Grand Prix circuit for the top players, and a year-round season of tournaments and international competitions. Badminton has become a major world sport.

BADMINTON IN THE UNITED STATES

In 1878, two New Yorkers, Bayard Clarke and E. Langdon Wilks, returned from overseas trips to India and England, respectively, having been exposed to badminton on their travels. With a friend, Oakley Rhinelander, they formed the Badminton Club of the City of New York, the oldest badminton club in the world in continuous existence. Badminton was primarily a society game for New York's upper crust until 1915, when intercity competitions with Boston's Badminton Club, formed in 1908, created a serious rivalry that continued through the 1920s.

By 1930, the game was spreading across the country and had become a serious, demanding sport for women and men. Clubs mushroomed on the Eastern seaboard, in the Midwest, and on the Pacific Coast. The Hollywood movie colony took to the game eagerly under the encouragement of a touring professional, George "Jess" Willard, who played exhibitions in movie houses across the country to packed houses and thereby did perhaps more than anyone to bring the game to the American people. Willard was followed on the national circuit by Ken Davidson, a Scotsman whose badminton comedy routines entertained millions in exhibitions in the 1930s and 1940s, and by Davidson's early partner, Hugh Forgie, a Canadian whose badminton-on-ice shows became world famous in the 1950s and 1960s. These three men combined great badminton talent with superb showmanship to spread the game in the United States and worldwide.

Through the leadership of some of Boston's best players, the American Badminton Association was formed in 1936, and the first national championships were held in 1937 in Chicago. One of the most famous names in world badminton appeared at the 1939 championships held in New York. An eighteen-year-old Californian, David G. Freeman, upset the defending champion Walter Kramer in the men's singles final to begin a winning streak that would last his ten-year badminton career. In 1949 he won the U.S. Championship, the All-England Championship, and all of his matches in the first Thomas Cup competitions. He then retired to continue his career as a neurosurgeon, and he is still considered perhaps the finest player the game has seen.

Following World War II, the first national junior championships were held in 1947. The development of badminton in schools and colleges led to the first national collegiate championships in 1970. The United States men's team made the Thomas Cup final rounds throughout the 1950s, and the women's team held the Uber Cup from 1957 until 1966; but the rapid development of the game across the world soon left the United States behind. Badminton continued to grow in the United States but at a much slower pace than during the prewar years. Golf, tennis, and the major professional sports came to the fore, while the popular misconception of badminton as only a leisurely recreation proved difficult to overcome. With the addition of badminton to the Olympic Games in 1992 and the success of the competition at the Atlanta games in 1996, it should only be a matter of time before the game will again become a sport of great popularity and recognition in the United States.

For more complete histories of badminton and for reproductions of the interesting drawings and paintings mentioned previously, the reader is referred to the books by Bernard Adams and Pat Davis listed in the references at the end of this book.

SUMMARY

- The game of badminton dates back to the first century B.C., with the development of the shuttlecock in China.
- For 500 years, battledore-shuttlecock was a pastime in Europe at all levels of society.
- Competitive badminton developed first in England and spread from there to Europe, America, and Asia.
- Badminton became an Olympic sport in 1992.

CHAPTER 2

FUNDAMENTALS
OF BADMINTON

OBJECTIVES

After reading this chapter, you should be able to do the following:

- Describe badminton's basic shots and strategies.
- Understand the rules for keeping score and the other basic rules of play.
- Describe the basic equipment required for badminton.

KEY TERMS

While reading this chapter, you will become familiar with the following terms:

▶ Clear ▶ Synthetic Shuttle

BASICS OF THE GAME

Badminton is a game played with rackets on a court divided by a net. It is distinguished from other racket sports, all of which use a ball, by two intriguing features: the use of a shuttlecock and that the shuttlecock must not touch the ground during a rally. The flight characteristics of the shuttlecock and the pace created by constant volleying combine to make badminton one of the most exciting sports to play and to watch.

BADMINTON FOR FITNESS

With the increased interest in physical health and vigor, badminton will play a more important role in the fitness programs so vital to the American citizen. The game is stimulating mentally and demanding physically, and it combines the values of individual and team sports. Badminton can be played by men, women, and children with only modest expense. That basic techniques are achievable and that beginners can learn to have lengthy rallies makes badminton enjoyable from the outset. Yet much training, practice, and dedication are required to perfect the skills, strength, speed, and stamina needed for becoming an excellent badminton player.

THE GAME

Badminton can be played indoors or outdoors and under artificial or natural lighting. All tournament play, however, is indoors because of the wind. There may be one player on a side (the singles game) or two players on a side (the doubles game). The shuttlecock does not bounce; it is played in the air, making for an exceptionally fast game requiring quick reflexes and superb conditioning. There is a wide variety of strokes in the game ranging from powerfully hit smashes (over 150 mph!) to delicately played drops.

Badminton is great fun because it is easy to learn. The racket is light and the shuttlecock can be hit back and forth in rallies even when the players possess a minimum of skill. Within a week or two after beginning to play, rallies and scoring can take place. There are few sports in which it is possible to feel like an "instant player." However, one should not assume that perfection of strokes and tournament caliber of play is by any means less difficult in badminton than in other sports.

A typical rally in badminton singles consists of a serve and repeated high deep shots hit to the baseline (**clears**), interspersed with drops. If and when a short clear or other type of "set-up" is forced, a smash wins the point. (All of these terms are described in the following chapters.) More often than not, an error (shuttle hit out-of-bounds or into the net) occurs rather than a positive playing finish to the rally. A player with increasing skill should commit fewer errors and make more winning plays to gain points. A player who is patient and commits few or no outright errors often wins, despite not being as naturally talented as the opponent, simply by waiting for the opponent to err.

In doubles, there are fewer clears and more low serves, drives, and net play. Again, the smash often terminates the point. As in singles, patience and the lack of unforced errors are most desirable. Team play and strategy in doubles are important, and often two players who have perfected their doubles system (rotating up and back on offense and defense) and choice of shots can prevail over two superior stroke players lacking in sound doubles teamwork and strategy.

SCORING

A badminton game consists of 15 points, except for women's singles in which a game is 11 points. The best of three games constitutes a match. Points can be scored only by the serving side. The sides change ends at the beginning of the second game and at the beginning of the third if a third game is necessary. In a 15-point game, ends are changed in the third game when the leading side reaches 8; in an 11-point game ends are changed when either side reaches 6. The side that wins a game serves first in the next game.

Unlike table tennis, a game does not need to be won when a player leads by 2 points. If the score becomes tied near the end of a game, the game may be lengthened by a procedure called "setting," described in chapter 3—Rules of Play, which also describes the serving rotation in singles and doubles, the various faults during play, and instructions for officiating.

EQUIPMENT FOR BADMINTON

To play the game of badminton, you need a court with a net, a racket, and a shuttlecock. The Laws of Badminton (see appendix A) contain formal requirements for this equipment. The most important of these specifications are presented in the following discussions.

▶ The Court

Measurements of the singles and doubles (combination) playing courts are shown in figures 2-1 and 2-2. The singles court is seventeen feet wide and forty-four feet long; the doubles court is three feet wider because of the two side alleys. There are also a center line, a short service line, and a doubles long service line.

The court is bisected laterally by a net elevated five feet above the ground at the center of the court and five feet one inch at the net posts, placed on the doubles

---

▶ Clear

A shot hit deep to the opponent's back boundary line. The *high clear* is a defensive shot, while the flatter *attacking clear* is used offensively.

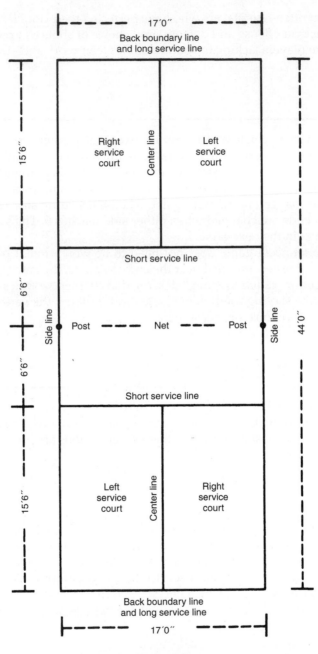

Singles court

FIGURE 2-1 Singles court.

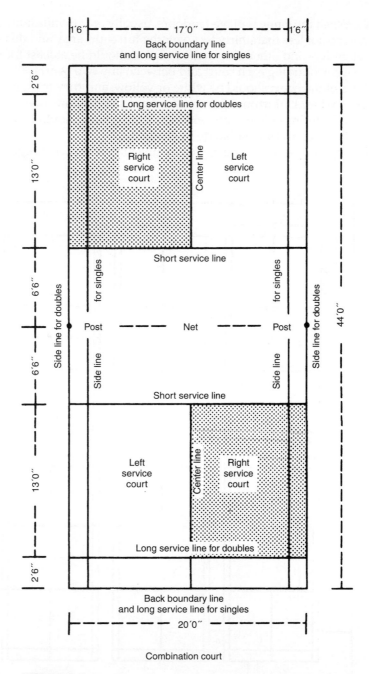

FIGURE 2-2 Combination court for singles and doubles.

sidelines. When the game is played indoors, usually on a gymnasium floor, the ceiling should be not less than thirty feet over the full court area, and this space should be free of girders and other obstructions. There should be at least four feet of clear floor space surrounding each court and between any two courts.

The lines of the court should be white or yellow, and they must be one and one-half inches wide. Unfortunately, many school gymnasium floors in the United States have badminton lines only one inch wide. These should be corrected eventually, and new courts should abide by the Laws.

An appropriate layout of courts in a gymnasium is shown in figure 2-3.

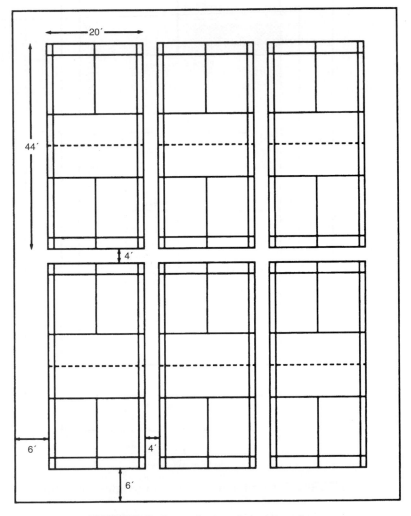

FIGURE 2-3 Court layout in gymnasium.

▶ Rackets

For many years, rackets were made entirely of wood. Shafts made of steel or fiberglass were introduced in the 1950s, but a revolution in materials technology has made wood rackets obsolete. Nearly all rackets of quality are now constructed of various blends of carbon, graphite, boron, aluminum, and steel. These rackets are light—around three and half ounces—and so strong that they can be strung much tighter than wooden rackets. Also, the modern rackets do not warp and hence need no press. The racket's overall dimensions cannot exceed twenty-seven inches by nine inches, and the length of the head cannot exceed eleven and one-half inches (figure 2-4).

Each racket manufacturer offers several models to suit each player's ability to play and pay; prices vary from $20 to $150. The racket is the most important item of equipment, therefore, novices should ask a more experienced player for help in selection. The cheaper rackets are heavier, and often more durable, but not as easy to swing quickly. The more expensive rackets are lighter and more flexible, but can suffer damage more easily in collisions with the floor or a partner's racket. Some experimenting is suggested before one chooses a racket.

The better known brands of rackets are Adidas, Black Knight, Carlton, Dunlop, I.S.I., Prince, Pro-Kennex, Slazenger, Sportcraft, Sugiyama, Victor, Yamaha, and Yonex. Few sporting goods stores in the United States carry a full line of rackets, although most will handle special orders in large quantities. It is often easier to order through dealers in badminton supplies (see chapter 9).

Rackets are strung with gut or some sort of synthetic string, like nylon. In the past, better players preferred gut, but the synthetics now equal the popularity of gut because the racket can be strung more tightly and because the synthetics cost less and last longer. A racket should be strung at between twenty and twenty-five lbs. tension, and a racket cover is suggested to protect the strings.

FIGURE 2-4 Rackets and shuttlecocks.

Rackets usually come with a handle grip made of leather or polyurethane. Replacement grips are available in these and other materials.

▶ Shuttlecocks

The traditional feathered shuttlecock is used in all major competitions. Various **synthetic shuttles** are acceptable and especially suitable for club and school play, if their flight characteristics are similar. The feathered shuttle must weigh from 4.74 to 5.50 grams and have sixteen feathers fixed in a cork base covered with a thin layer of leather or similar material. The required dimensions of the shuttle are given in the laws (see appendix A). These requirements give the shuttle its unusual, although predictable, flight patterns.

In synthetic shuttles, the feathers are replaced by a "skirt" of some manufactured material, but such shuttles must meet the specifications of the feather shuttle. A good synthetic shuttle costs slightly less than the feather shuttle and usually lasts longer.

Both types of shuttles, but especially the feather shuttles, will last much longer if they are humidified. This keeps the shuttle from drying, becoming brittle, and thus breaking. This is simple to do: glue a small piece of sponge on the inside of the cap of the tube that holds the shuttles and keep the sponge damp.

To insure that the game takes the same form whenever and wherever it is played, it is imperative to standardize a shuttle's speed. A profound difference in the type of game results if a fast shuttle instead of a slow shuttle is selected for use. The heavier the shuttle, the faster it flies. The shuttle also flies faster under conditions of increased temperature and altitude. Weights of manufactured shuttles therefore vary to meet conditions at a particular time; some manufacturers merely classify shuttles as slow, medium, or fast. Under normal conditions, a medium (5.1 grams) shuttle is appropriate. Each time the game is played, the shuttle should function at the same speed regardless of atmospheric conditions. The speed of the shuttle can be altered by crimping the stalks of the feathers near the tip and bending them slightly—outward to slow the shuttle and inward to speed it up.

The testing of a shuttle's speed takes place at the beginning of a match. The test is made by having a player strike the shuttle with a full underhand stroke from a spot directly above one back boundary line in a direction parallel to the sideline and at an upward angle. It must land in a three-foot range centered on the opposite doubles long service line (see figure 2-5).

The better known brands of feather shuttles are Black Knight, Carlton, Flying, HL, Rackets International, RSL, Sportcraft, Victor, and Yonex. The price for a tube of a dozen varies from fifteen dollars to twenty dollars. Synthetic shuttles are manufactured by most of these companies. Some synthetic shuttles, and even some feathered shuttles, are available in yellow for better visibility in halls with light-colored walls. It is important to buy better quality synthetics, which cost about twelve dol-

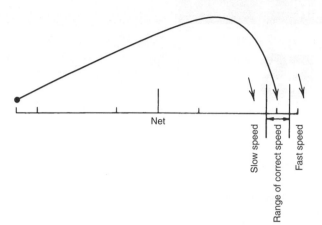

Net

Slow speed

Range of correct speed

Fast speed

FIGURE 2-5 Shuttle test.

lars per dozen, because the cheaper ones seldom have correct speed or satisfactory flight characteristics.

SUMMARY

- Though badminton is easy to learn, championship level badminton requires great speed, strength, and stamina.
- The basic shots of badminton—clears, drops, and smashes—are used in different combinations for singles and doubles.
- A badminton game is played to 15 points in all events except women's singles, in which a game is 11 points.
- The basic equipment for badminton consists of a court with a net, a racket, and a shuttlecock.

▶ **Synthetic shuttle**
A less expensive shuttle compared to the traditional feather shuttle.

CHAPTER 3

RULES
OF PLAY

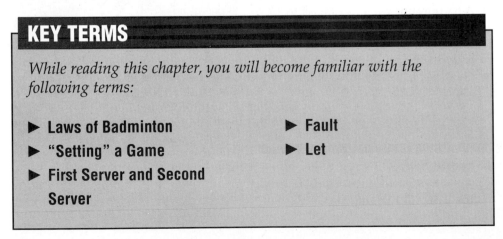

OBJECTIVES

After reading this chapter, you should be able to do the following:

- Describe the basic Laws of Badminton regarding serving, scoring, faults, and lets.
- Follow the commonly accepted rules for court behavior, for informal play and tournaments.
- Understand the requirements for officiating and the responsibilities of court officials.

KEY TERMS

While reading this chapter, you will become familiar with the following terms:

▶ Laws of Badminton
▶ "Setting" a Game
▶ First Server and Second Server

▶ Fault
▶ Let

The International Badminton Federation (IBF) annually publishes a statute book containing the **Laws of Badminton** and interpretations and revisions of the laws. USA Badminton adopts these laws for badminton play in this country, and it also publishes a handbook containing them. The Laws of Badminton are reproduced in full in appendix A, as they were modified in 1998. No changes in the laws will occur until 2002. The summary in this chapter of the rules of play will suffice for school, college, and recreational badminton. The rules on playing equipment are summarized in chapter 2.

SUMMARY OF THE LAWS

▶ Players

1. Players are those persons taking part in the game: one player on a side in singles, two players on a side in doubles. The side that has the serve is called the "in" side and the opposing side, the "out" side.

▶ Toss

2. Before play begins, the opposing sides shall toss a coin or a racket. The winner of the toss shall have the option of serving first, not serving first, or choosing ends of the court. The side losing the toss shall then have a choice of the remaining alternatives. Decisions made at this time can be important. One end of the court may be more desirable than the other because of lighting arrangements, floor conditions, and location of spectators.

▶ Serving and Scoring

3. Play is started by an underhand serve and a side can score only when serving. Each time an exchange or rally is won while serving, a point is recorded. If the rally is lost while serving, neither side is awarded a point. Instead, the right to serve is relinquished, and the serve passes to the opponents (singles) or to the next player in rotation (doubles).

▶ Laws of Badminton

The International Badminton Federation (IBF) annually publishes a statute book with these laws. USA Badminton adopts these laws for badminton played in the United States.

4. Doubles and men's singles games consist of 15 points; women's singles, 11 points. Peculiar to the scoring system is the term "**setting.**" This is a method of extending the length of a game if the game is tied. In particular, when the score becomes tied at "14-all" in a 15-point game, the side that reached 14 first has the option of "setting" the game to a total of 17 points, so that the side that scores 3 points first wins the game. In women's singles, the 11-point game may be set to 13 points at "10-all," again so that the side that scores 3 points first wins the game. See figure 3-1.

Points in Game	Score Tied at	Game may be set to
11	10	13 points
15	14	17 points

The side that reached the tied score first has the option of setting or not setting the game. If the side elects not to set the game, then the conventional number

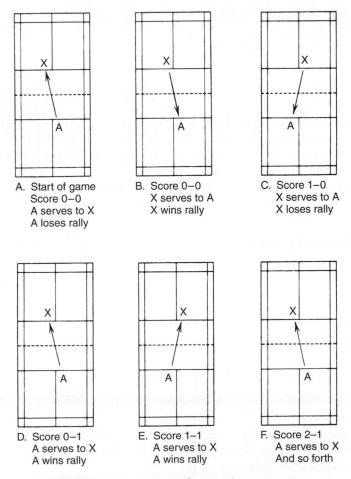

FIGURE 3-1 Typical singles serving sequence.

of points completes the game. For example, the score of a match could thus be 15–14, 16–17, 17–15.

5. A match shall consist of the best of three games. The players change ends at the beginning of the second game and at the beginning of the third game, if a third game is necessary. In the third game, players change ends when either player first reaches 8 in a game of 15 points or 6 in a game of 11 points. The object of this change of ends is to try to give both players equal time on both ends of the court. If players forget to change ends, they should change as soon as their mistake is discovered.

6. An *inning* is a term of service, and there may be any number of innings because many rallies are played for which no points are scored.

7. A serve is deemed completed as soon as the shuttle is struck by the server's racket. Unlike the serve in tennis, only one serve is allowed a player to put the shuttle into play.

8. A shot falling inside the boundaries or directly on a line is considered good.

9. When any unusual occurrence interferes with the play, a "let" (replay of the point) can be invoked. This happens, for example, if a stray shuttle from a nearby court interferes or if a line judge or umpire is unable to make a decision on a particular shot.

▶ Serving Rotation

10. *Singles* In singles, the players serve from and receive in the right service court when the server's score is an even number. When the server's score is an odd number, the players serve from and receive in the left service court. See figure 3-1 for a typical serving sequence.

11. *Doubles* In doubles, the service rotation is determined by the score and by positions on the court at the start of a game. In this way, badminton is different from other racket sports in which the rotation is fixed. Figure 3-2 illustrates this process in a typical serving sequence. The side serving first in a game has only one turn at serve. The server delivers the first serve in a game from the right service court to the receiver in the right service court on the opposing side and then alternates service courts as long as rallies are won. The receiving side does not change courts. After this first inning, *both* players on a side have a turn at serve before the serve passes to the other side. In each successive inning, the "**first server**" is the player who by the team's score is correctly in the right service court when his or her team regains the serve. The first server

▶ **"Setting" a Game**
Method of extending a tied game by increasing the number of points necessary to win. Side reaching the tied score first has option of setting.

▶ **First Server**
In doubles, the player who serves first for a side during a particular inning.

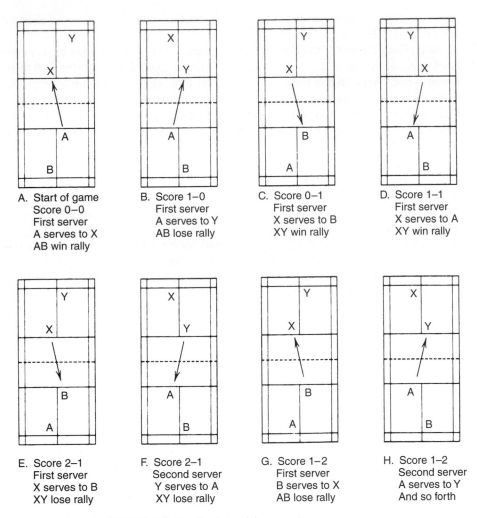

A. Start of game
Score 0–0
First server
A serves to X
AB win rally

B. Score 1–0
First server
A serves to Y
AB lose rally

C. Score 0–1
First server
X serves to B
XY win rally

D. Score 1–1
First server
X serves to A
XY win rally

E. Score 2–1
First server
X serves to B
XY lose rally

F. Score 2–1
Second server
Y serves to A
XY lose rally

G. Score 1–2
First server
B serves to X
AB lose rally

H. Score 1–2
Second server
A serves to Y
And so forth

FIGURE 3-2 Typical doubles serving sequence.

serves until a rally is lost; and then the serve passes to the "**second server,**" without courts being changed. The second server continues to serve, alternating courts, until a rally is lost, and then the serve goes to the other side.

Thus, when the serving side's score is an even number, the server should be standing in the service court (right or left) in which he or she began the game. When the side's score is an odd number, the server should be in the opposite service court. The same applies to the receiver and the receiving side's score. During the serve, the partners of the server and receiver may stand anywhere on the court. After the serve is delivered, players on both sides may take any positions on the court they wish.

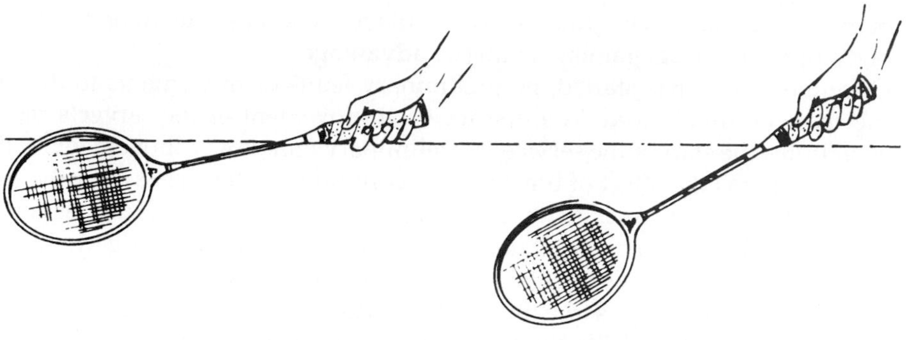

FIGURE 3-3 Illegal serve, legal serve.

▶ Faults

The Laws of Badminton include certain rules that cannot be violated without penalty. If any violation of the following laws occurs, it is a **fault** on the offending side. If the receiving side faults, the serving side scores a point. If the serving side faults, no point is scored and the serve passes to the next appropriate server.

▶ Faults During Serving and Receiving

12. A serve must be an underhand stroke, and the entire shuttle must be below the server's waist on contact. To insure that the serve is an underhand stroke, the shaft of the racket must point downward at the time of contact to such an extent that the entire head of the racket is discernibly below the hand and fingers holding the racket (figure 3-3 and appendix A, diagram D).
13. A player's feet must be stationary and in the correct court upon delivery of the serve. It is not a fault if the server takes up a stance and then takes one step forward, provided the step is completed before the start of the forward motion of the racket.
14. The server should not serve until the receiver is ready. A receiver attempting to return the serve, however, is judged ready. A receiver who is not ready should not attempt a return but rather let the shuttle fall to the court and then tell the server or the umpire that he or she was not ready, in which case the serve shall

---

▶ **Second Server**
In doubles, the partner who has second turn at serving for a side during a particular inning.

▶ **Fault**
A violation of the playing rules, either in serving, in receiving, or during play.

be delivered again. This rule keeps the player who has a tendency to hurry one's opponent from gaining an undue advantage.

15. Once the service has started, no preliminary feints or movements to distract the receiver are allowed. The first forward movement of the server's racket constitutes the start of the service. A preliminary feint is any movement by the server that has the effect of breaking the continuity of the serve after the two players have taken their ready positions to begin the point. Such action is termed a balk, and a balk is a fault. It is also a fault if the server delays hitting the shuttle for so long as to be unfair to the receiver.

16. If a player attempting a serve misses the shuttle completely, it is a fault.

17. A serve that lands outside the boundaries of the service court is a fault. See figure 2-2 for service court boundaries.

18. A player may not serve or receive out of turn or from the wrong court. The consequences of an infraction of this law depend upon when the mistake is discovered. If the player who commits one of these serving or receiving errors wins the rally, and the mistake is immediately discovered, a **let** is called. If the player at fault loses the rally or if the mistake is not discovered before the next point commences, the mistake stands; that is, no let. In that case, the already altered serving and receiving order is not changed until the end of the game, regardless of which team won or lost the rally.

19. The receiver's partner may not strike a serve meant for the receiver.

▶ Faults During Play

20. If the shuttle falls outside the boundaries, passes through or under the net, fails to pass the net, touches the roof or side walls, or touches a person or the clothing of a person, the rally ceases and the player committing the fault is penalized. However, a serve hitting the top of the net and going into the correct service court is legal and "in play." Some gymnasiums or halls may have low beams, ropes, or other obstructions hanging over the court. In such cases the local association may establish a ground rule to the effect that a shuttle hitting the obstruction would be considered not a fault but a let. If careful judgment by an experienced person is not made in this case, a player might intentionally hit the obstruction when it appeared that the point was going to be lost. If an obstruction can be hit deliberately, the fault rule is usually enforced. An unusual and uncommon situation develops when a shuttle passes the net outside of the net post and then flies into the court. This is the only case in which the shuttle can go below the net level and still be legal.

21. A player may not reach over the net to contact a shuttle. One may, however, contact the shuttle on one's own side of the net and follow through with the racket on the opponent's side, providing the net is not touched.

22. When the shuttle is "in play," a player may not touch the net or the net posts with one's body, racket, or clothing. If the net is hit following a stroke and after the shot has struck the floor, a fault does not result because the shuttle is not "in play" after it strikes the floor.

23. The shuttle may not be hit twice in succession before being returned to the opponent. This rule prevents setting the shuttle up to oneself or to one's partner.

24. The shuttle may not be caught on the racket and then slung during the execution of the stroke. Commonly called "carry," "sling," or "throw," this fault is difficult to detect, and it is often committed unintentionally by beginners because of poor timing. More advanced players seldom commit this fault outright, but occasionally when a deceptive technique is attempted the infraction may occur. When a "carry" is committed, the shuttle's speed and direction are changed. This naturally handicaps the receiver of such a shot, and a player should not be penalized by another player's poor technique. The rule, then, is an essential one, and any player at fault should immediately call "No Shot."

25. A fault is called when a player is hit by the shuttle whether one is standing inside or outside the court boundaries. It is surprising to many players to realize that if they are able to hit their opponent with the shuttle, the point is theirs! This, however, is more difficult to accomplish than it sounds.

26. If a shuttle is hit into the net or caught in the net on the striker's side, it is not "in play." If the shuttle goes over the net, but catches on the other side, a let results. The point is replayed because the player on whose side the shuttle was caught did not have a fair chance of returning the shuttle. If the player attempted to play the shuttle that was caught in the net and in doing so hit the net, then a "fault," rather that a let, would be called.

27. A player may not step on the opponent's side of the net if this obstructs or distracts the opponent.

28. A player may not intentionally hold the racket near the net, obstructing the opponent's stroke, hoping that the shuttle will happen to rebound from the racket into the opponent's court. This occasionally happens when a player close to the net tries to defend against a smash. On the other hand, a racket held in front of one's face for protection is a good maneuver; any resulting shot is acceptable.

29. A player may not "unsight" another player during service. This rule, applicable only in doubles, means that the server's partner must not stand in front of the server in such a way that the receiver cannot see the shuttle about to be served. If this situation occurs, the receiver tells the server or the umpire, before the shuttle is served, that the shuttle cannot be seen. An adjustment of the starting positions is then made by the serving side.

30. Play must be continuous. A player therefore may not leave the court, receive advice, or rest at any time from the start to the conclusion of the match, except

▶ **Let**
A legitimate cessation of play to allow a rally to be replayed.

during the intervals described below. The umpire shall judge whether this rule has been broken, and a player violating this rule may be warned, faulted, or disqualified. A ninety-second interval between the first and second games is allowed for a player to rest on court and receive coaching from the edge of the court. A five-minute interval between the second and third games is allowed if any player requests it; during this interval a player may leave the court and receive coaching.

UNWRITTEN RULES

Badminton, like all sports, has unwritten as well as written rules. The common courtesies, or etiquette, of badminton commence with your first introduction to the game.

▶ Conduct on the Court

During the warm up:
1. Agree on a correct shuttle for use.
2. Hit the shuttle to your opponent so he or she can also warm up.
   During the match:
1. If you are serving, be sure your opponent is ready before you serve, and call the score if there is no umpire.
2. In the absence of court officials, call faults on yourself promptly and fairly.
3. If there are no line judges, make line decisions correctly; do not ask spectators for help with line decisions and avoid repeatedly suggesting replays.
4. Retrieve shuttles on your side of the net and those nearest you. When you return the shuttle, hit it to your opponent when he or she is ready, and do not just shove it under the net.
5. Ask your opponent first if you wish to change or modify the shuttle.
6. Avoid abusive language and racket throwing.
7. Play at your best even if your opponent does not have your expertise. It is insulting to your opponent to do otherwise.
   Following the match:
1. Shake hands and thank your opponent and any court officials.

▶ Tournament Conduct

1. Fill out the tournament entry blank accurately and completely, and return it on time.
2. Plan to arrive at the tournament well before the time of your first match. Report to the tournament desk upon arrival at the tournament, verify the time of your match, and check your opponent's name and the court number.
3. Avoid being late on court for your match. Do not risk being defaulted.

4. Do your stretching and warm up before going on the court, so that you need at most five minutes of rallying before beginning.
5. After the match, thank the umpire and find out the time of your next match. If there is no umpire, report the score to the tournament desk.
6. After the tournament, write a thank-you note to the tournament chair and to any other hosts you may have had.

▶ A Final Word

In all competitive play, learning to win and lose gracefully is essential. Don't blame your defeat or poor play on some trivial matter or excuse. Keep your thoughts to yourself, analyze your play, and determine to increase your abilities.

▶ Officiating

The officials needed to conduct a match are an umpire, a service judge, and ten line judges. National, international, and world championship matches require this full complement of officials. Locally, twelve officials are rarely available until the final round. State and school matches are often played without any officials, in which case the players keep score and conduct the match.

▶ Duties of the Officials

The umpire conducts the match, calls the score, rules on receiving faults, and enforces the laws of badminton. The service judge rules on service faults (this chapter, items 12–16). The line judges determine if the shuttle is "in" (inside or on the line) or "out" (outside the line). If the service judge or line judges cannot make a decision, the umpire may do so, but the umpire may not overrule a decision of these judges.

For those particularly interested in this facet of the game, information can be found in the USAB Rule Book or the IBF Statute Book (see the references at end of the book).

Figure 3-4 shows the position of officials for a match. U refers to the umpire, SJ to the service judge, and L to line judges.

▶ Conduct of the Match

1. Only an official has the privilege of communicating with the players. The two exceptions are during the ninety-second interval that comes at the end of the

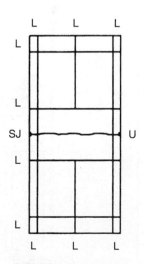

FIGURE 3-4 Location of officials on court.

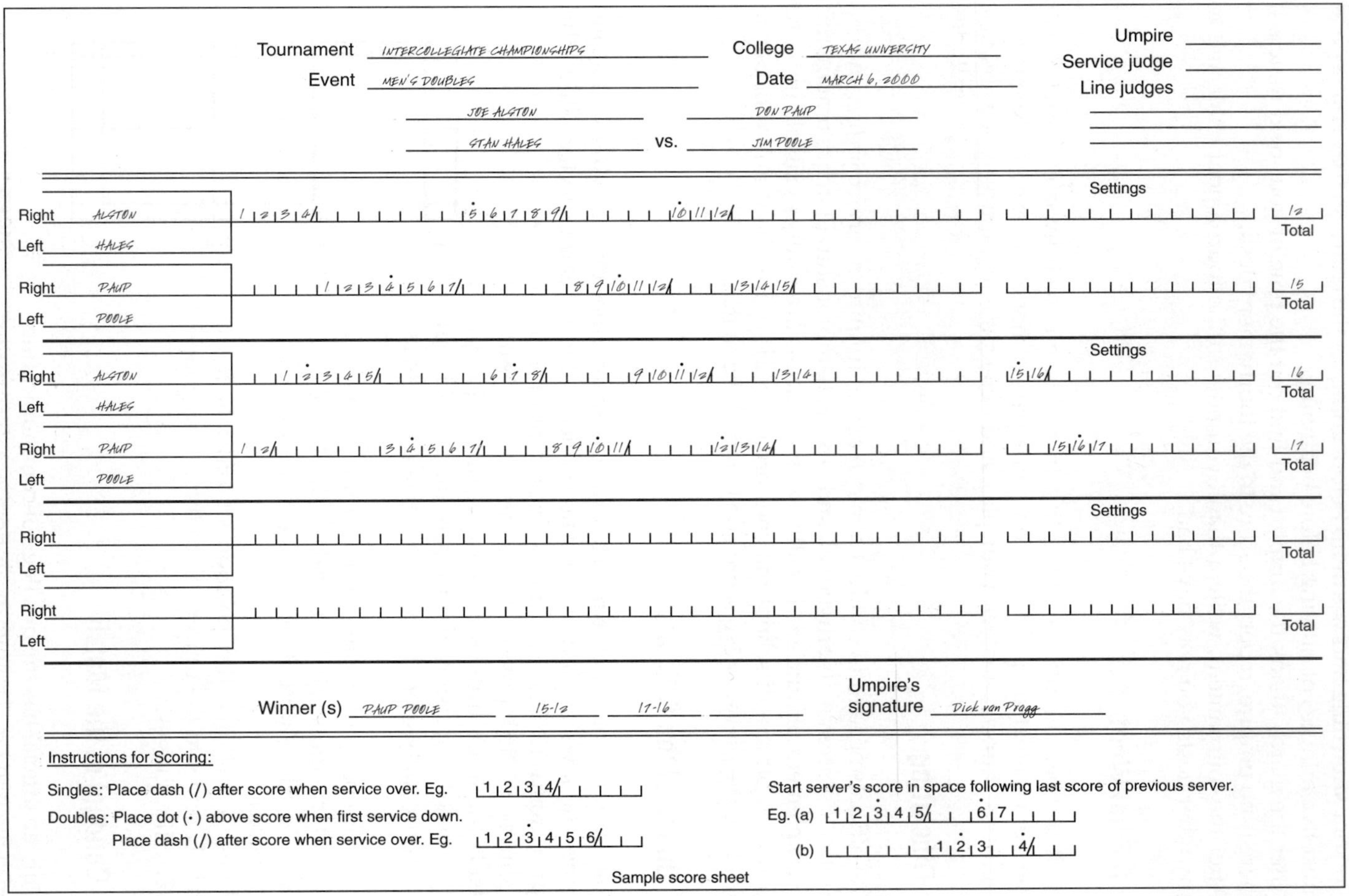

Tournament _INTERCOLLEGIATE CHAMPIONSHIPS_   College _TEXAS UNIVERSITY_
Event _MEN'S DOUBLES_   Date _MARCH 6, 2000_

JOE ALSTON
STAN HALES   vs.   _DON PAUP_
JIM POOLE

Umpire _____
Service judge _____
Line judges _____

Settings

	Total
Right ALSTON	12
Left HALES	
Right PAUP	15
Left POOLE	

Settings

	Total
Right ALSTON	16
Left HALES	
Right PAUP	17
Left POOLE	

Settings

	Total
Right	
Left	
Right	
Left	

Winner(s) _PAUP POOLE_   _15-12_   _17-16_

Umpire's signature _Dick von Pragg_

Instructions for Scoring:

Singles: Place dash (/) after score when service over. Eg.   1,2,3,4/

Doubles: Place dot (•) above score when first service down.
Place dash (/) after score when service over. Eg.   1,2,3,4,5,6/

Start server's score in space following last score of previous server.

Eg. (a)   1,2,3,4,5/   6,7

(b)   1,2,3,4/

Sample score sheet

FIGURE 3-5 Sample score sheet.

first game and the five-minute interval at the end of the second game if a third game is required to determine the winner of the match.

2. Applause at any time is welcomed but spectators should refrain from making sudden noises while the shuttle is in play.
3. Decisions of the line judges are final. If no line judges are available, the umpire will inform the players how the decisions on the line will be made.
   Figure 3-5 is a sample score sheet used by the umpires.

SUMMARY

- The International Badminton Federation (IBF) annually publishes a statute book containing the Laws of Badminton. Refer to appendix A for the full, detailed version of the laws.
- The common courtesies, or etiquette, of badminton start from the first introduction to the game. Depending on the level and location of competitive play, officials are not always available. Whatever the situation, honesty and good temperament will help everyone enjoy the game.

CHAPTER 4

SKILLS FOR EVERY PLAYER—PRELIMINARIES

OBJECTIVES

After reading this chapter, you should know the following:

- How to warm up.
- How to grip your racket.
- Where to position yourself on the court.
- How to stand when awaiting returns.
- How to move about the court.

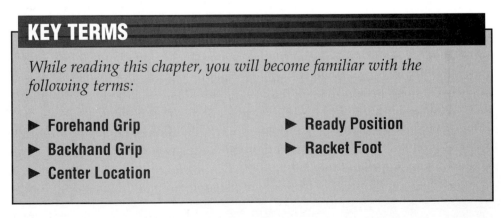

KEY TERMS

While reading this chapter, you will become familiar with the following terms:

▶ Forehand Grip
▶ Backhand Grip
▶ Center Location

▶ Ready Position
▶ Racket Foot

Before a beginning badminton player learns the basic shots that are useful in a game of singles or doubles, as well as the stroking techniques employed to produce these shots, it is also necessary to acquire some associated skills that accompany good stroke technique. This chapter describes the skills prerequisite to effective shot production, and chapter 5 describes the basic strokes and shots themselves. Chapter 7 contains instruction on more advanced strokes and shots that should be learned only when you have become familiar with the techniques of this chapter and chapter 5.

HOW TO WARM UP

It takes time to stretch and warm up properly for badminton. Get off to a good start by warming up sufficiently before going on court. Especially when playing competitively, you should increase your body temperature for maximum performance. Before going on court, do the following:

1. Stretch out the muscles and tendons of your legs, stomach, back, and arms by a series of slow exercises while sitting and standing: toe touches, trunk twists, arm circles, and so on.
2. Swing the racket while it is still in its cover, simulating the various badminton strokes, especially clears and drives. Start slowly, gradually speeding up the swing.
3. Bounce on your feet and run in place to get your legs limber.
4. Practice quick starts with footwork similar to that on court.
5. Take quick, short sprints—forward, backward, side to side, and diagonally.

HOW TO GRIP YOUR RACKET

Most badminton strokes are executed with either a **forehand** or **backhand** grip. Strokes made overhead or on the right side of the body require a forehand grip. Strokes made on the left side of the body require a backhand grip. (These suggestions and instructions and others of a similar nature throughout the book pertain to right-handed players. Left-handed players should in each case use the side opposite to that cited.)

▶ **Forehand Grip**
Refers to strokes played on the racket side of the body.

▶ **Backhand Grip**
Refers to strokes played on the non-racket side of the body (i.e., with the racket across the body).

FOREHAND GRIP

Examine your badminton racket handle. It has eight sides or bevels. The top bevel is the side of the handle visible when the racket head is held at right angles to the ground, as shown in figure 4-1. Here are five points to remember in holding the racket for this grip:

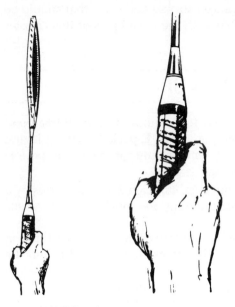

FIGURE 4-1 Forehand grip.

1. The point of the V formed by your thumb and forefinger is at the left edge of the top bevel of the handle (figure 4-1).
2. Hold the racket in your fingers, not just in your palm like a hammer. Lay the racket across your fingers and palm, and let your little finger maintain a firm hold (figure 4-2).
3. Spread your fingers so they are comfortable, particularly the forefinger and middle finger. Use your thumb and forefinger to control the racket.
4. Hold the racket near the end of the handle. This allows more wrist action. Do not let the butt of the handle extend beyond the heel of your hand,

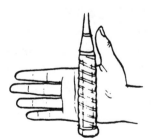

Wrong

Right

FIGURE 4-2 Use of the fingers on the grip.

except in special circumstances when "choking up" is necessary for quick response.

5. When you execute "power" shots, hold the racket firmly at impact. On "touch" shots, hold the racket more loosely.

To get a comfortable feeling it may be necessary to adjust this basic grip by spreading or closing your fingers, by moving your hand closer to the end, or by resting the end of the handle at a comfortable place on the heel of your hand.

Remember: The position of the V should not be changed.

BACKHAND GRIP

For this grip (for shots played on the left side of the body), remember these three points (figure 4-3):

1. Turn your hand counterclockwise until the point of the V is on the top angled left bevel.
2. On drives and clears, place the ball (or first joint) of your thumb flat against the back bevel of the handle. This position gives the support necessary for power and depth.
3. Drops and net shots require control rather than power, so it is not necessary to have your thumb flat. It may rest across the back bevel as it does on the forehand.

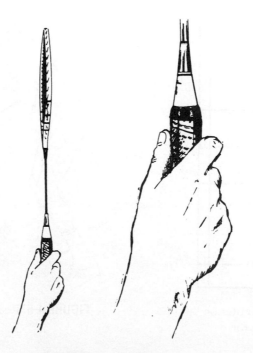

FIGURE 4-3 Backhand grip.

WHERE TO POSITION YOURSELF ON THE COURT

The **center location** is your basic position in singles play. This is the location on the court from which you are able to reach most shots easily. Here, you command the best area for any maneuver.

The center location is halfway between the net and back boundary line and on the center line, halfway between the sidelines (figure 4-4).

Your opponent will try to draw you from this basic center position by directing the shuttle to a corner. Your strategy is to retrieve the corner shots but return quickly to the center position.

HOW TO STAND WHEN AWAITING RETURNS

To ready yourself for each of your opponent's shots, practice these five points consciously, until they become habit (figure 4-5):

1. Take a position in the center of the court. Stand alertly with your weight evenly distributed on the balls of your feet.
2. Stand with your feet side by side and apart just enough to give good balance, but not so far apart that movement is restricted.

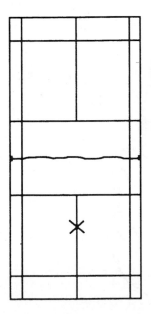

FIGURE 4-4 Center or base position for singles.

FIGURE 4-5 Ready position.

3. Relax your body, and flex your knees slightly; do not be stiff and upright. Be ready for instantaneous action.
4. Carry both your arms in front of your body, with the racket acting almost as a shield. Hold the racket head up about shoulder height and away from you to allow a swift stroke.
5. Concentrate on the shuttle as it leaves your opponent's racket, and try to determine the direction of the shot. As soon as you determine the direction, move your feet and pivot your body by the time the shuttle crosses the net.

All players vary the **ready position** somewhat to suit their own style and comfort. Champions adjust it to give them the greatest mobility and quickness. Quickness refers not only to feet and hands but to eyes and brains as well. The shuttle has such a short distance to travel that it will come swiftly and offer you little time to execute the fundamentals.

In badminton no time is available to pause and survey the situation. Even in doubles, where your partner covers half the court, you must be ready for every shot. Points are made because opponents have neither the time nor the reflexes to get their rackets in position to return the shuttle.

HOW TO MOVE ABOUT THE COURT

To get within reach of the shuttlecock and to conserve energy in the process, good footwork is essential. Powerful and deceptive strokes are of little use if a player is not in the correct place soon enough to stroke the shuttle effectively.

ESSENTIALS OF GOOD FOOTWORK

1. The beginning of good footwork is an alert starting position. Keep the body ready to move in any direction by flexing the knees slightly with your weight on the forward part of your feet. Think "ready." A stiff upright stance does not permit speed.
2. Badminton footwork is best described as "springing sideways and gliding to the shuttle." Keep your feet close to the floor.
3. It is important not to be moving when your opponent hits the shuttle. If you cannot get completely back to the center of the court, pause where you are before your opponent hits the shuttle.

▶ **Center Location**
The basic position in singles play; the location on court from which you are able to reach most shots easily.

▶ **Ready Position**
An alert body position enabling the player to make quick movement in any direction.

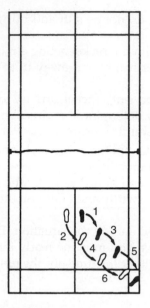

FIGURE 4-6 Footwork to deep forehand corner.

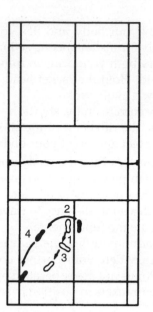

FIGURE 4-7 Footwork to deep backhand corner.

▶ Moving to the Baseline

4. To prepare for a forehand overhead stroke in the deep right court, lead with your right foot and take gliding steps diagonally back to the corner. Finish with your left side partially turned toward the net. Your left foot is forward as you hit (figure 4-6).
5. To prepare for a backhand stroke from the deep left court, turn on the left foot and stride diagonally back to the corner with your back partially turned to the net. Your right foot is out in front of you, pointed sideways or diagonally to the rear corner (figure 4-7).

▶ Moving to the Net

6. To move to either corner at net, push off with your left foot and lead with your right. The second step is a short shuffle step with your left foot, and the third step lands you with the right foot in front (figures 4-8 and 4-9).

The right foot is the **racket foot** in badminton. Unlike tennis, most shots are played "off" the right foot (that is, the right leg and foot have the weight on them at the moment of contact) even when playing shots on the right side of the court. This allows for better reach, without getting too far from the center of the court. After

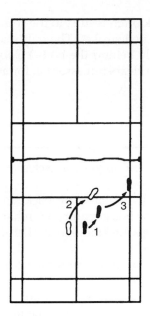

FIGURE 4-8 Footwork to front forehand corner.

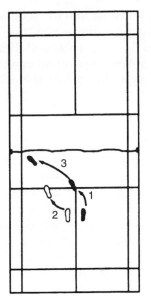

FIGURE 4-9 Footwork to front backhand corner.

playing the shot, let your left leg share the load by using it to push off back toward center position.

As your footwork skills become more proficient, the number of steps from center to all parts of the court can be determined. The footwork then becomes a pattern. Learning to judge whether shuttle is going out of bounds on the baseline and sidelines is made easier when the footwork becomes measured. The easiest part of badminton footwork is running forward. The basic waiting position is in the center of the court, therefore, backward and sideward steps are also required. Moving backward is called "backpedaling." It is a skill demanded in other sports, too. The football quarterback backpedals almost every time he takes the ball from the center.

So it is with the badminton player. Keep your head and eyes forward at all times. If you have to turn and run with your back to the net, you will not have enough time to turn again to stroke the shuttle.

Good footwork combined with early anticipation of the direction and depth of the shuttlecock should place the player *behind* the shuttle. This enables a move

▶ **Racket Foot**

The foot most shots are played "off" of (i.e., the right leg and foot have the

weight on them at the moment of contact).

forward and a hit into the shot. Sluggish footwork often results in the shuttle getting behind the player, resulting in a poorly executed stroke. (The only exception to this is the deep backhand, best hit from slightly behind the body.) Good footwork is not only important in returning high deep clears but essential for an effective return of a high deep serve.

SUMMARY

- Before play begins, it is important to stretch, warm up your muscles, and practice swinging the racket.
- Badminton strokes are executed with either a forehand or backhand grip. Strokes made overhead or on the right side of the body require a forehand grip, while strokes on the left side of the body require a backhand grip. (Left-handed players should use the side opposite to that cited.)
- In singles, players should be in the ready position in the center location of the court during rallies, in between shots.
- Badminton calls for good footwork to move side-to-side and forward and backward on the court. It is important to "plant" your racket foot at the moment of contacting the shuttle.

Assessment 4-1

Name   Section   Date

1. How is the backhand grip for a net shot changed to perform a backhand high clear? Why is this change in hand position advocated?
2. Practice moving from center court to the right and left sidelines and to the baseline until you are consistent in the number of steps taken for a given direction. How many steps do you require to play the shuttle from each of the boundary lines?
3. In playing a shot from the right corner at net, which foot should be forward as you stroke the shuttlecock, and why?

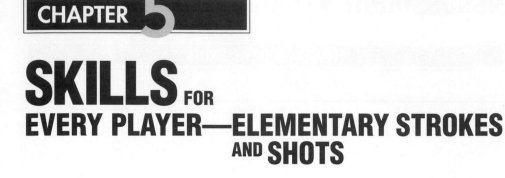

CHAPTER 5

SKILLS FOR EVERY PLAYER—ELEMENTARY STROKES AND SHOTS

OBJECTIVES

After reading this chapter, you should know the fundamental stroking techniques for the following basic shots:

- Underhand strokes—the serve and the underhand clear and drop.
- Overhead strokes—the clear, the drop, and the smash.
- Sidearm stroke—the drive.
- Net play.

KEY TERMS

While reading this chapter, you will become familiar with the following terms:

▶ High Serve

▶ Low Serve

▶ High Clear and Attacking Clear

▶ Pronation

▶ Angle of the Racket Face

▶ Hairpin Drop

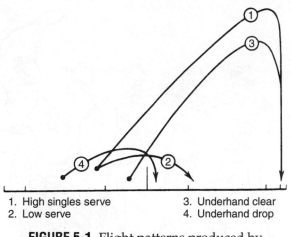

1. High singles serve   3. Underhand clear
2. Low serve   4. Underhand drop

FIGURE 5-1 Flight patterns produced by underhand strokes.

UNDERHAND STROKES

Underhand strokes are those in which the contact point and the head of the racket are below the level of the hand. The contact point is below net level, which necessitates an upward stroke (figure 5-1).

THE SERVE

Begin play with the serve, an underhand stroke. Play it underhand forehand or underhand backhand, although underhand forehand is the usual method. The shaft of the racket must point downward so that the whole of the head of the racket is discernibly below the hand holding the racket (figures 3-3 and 5-2).

► Basic Singles Serve—The High Serve

1. Take a comfortable position in the court about three feet behind the short service line and to the right or left of the center line.
2. Stand with your feet spread but not so far apart that you cannot move quickly. Your left foot should be in advance of your right foot.

► **High Serve**
The basic singles serve used in badminton.

FIGURE 5-2 Serve.

3. Both feet must remain in contact with the floor until you contact the shuttle. Once you put your racket in motion to serve, neither foot may slide until after the shuttle is struck.
4. Hold the shuttle at the base between your thumb and forefinger of your left hand (or use both fore- and middle fingers). Extend your left arm forward about level with your shoulders (figure 5-2).
5. Hold the racket with a forehand grip with your wrist cocked. Bring the racket behind your body at about waist level. This is the starting position. Then drop or toss the shuttle in front of you.
6. Swing the racket forward, uncock the wrist, and let the racket and shuttle meet ahead of your body at approximately knee level.
7. Rapidly rotate the forearm and wrist inward immediately prior to contact. Most strokes in badminton are made with a similar rotating movement.
8. The follow-through goes in the direction that you intend the shuttle to go, that is, high and deep. Avoid bringing the racket up to the shuttle. Let the shuttle drop. Otherwise an outright miss or a poor shot will result (figure 5-3).

▶ The Low Serve

The **low serve** is used primarily in doubles and with great variation. It is also used as a change of pace in singles. The grips and stance are usually the same as for the singles serve, but the racket pattern and use of the wrist vary widely. Of all the strokes in badminton, the low serve technique has the most variables. The swing is often shortened and the stroke made almost entirely with your forearm guiding the shuttle. Most players prefer an exceptionally firm wrist believing it

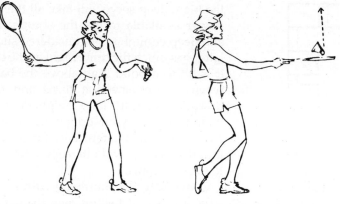

Holding shuttle by feathers   Contacting shuttle too high

FIGURE 5-3 Mistakes most commonly made with
the serve.

gives more control. This is one stroke you must experiment with to find the style
best suited for you. Try for accuracy in having the shuttle go over the top of the net
with minimum clearance. If your low serve forces the receiver to hit up it is a
highly successful serve. If the receiver "rushes" your low serve and is able to hit it
on the downswing, change your technique and practice it more.

▶ Placement Areas

The serve can be directed high or low, short or long. Figure 5-4 shows the
specific areas within the service court to which the shuttle can be served most
effectively.

In singles there should be no noticeable difference in the way you produce low
and high serves, as here again deception is important to keep your opponent in
doubt as to which it will be (and off balance). Basically, the high serve is used more
often in singles and the low serve more often in doubles. Occasionally mixing
them keeps your opponent uncertain and unable to predict your pattern. It is imperative that you serve well, as serving gives you the opportunity to score.

Even though somewhat alike in production, the low and high serves are different. They can be compared with the drop and clear in wrist action and needed
power. The low serve takes little power and is almost guided over the net whereas

▶ **Low Serve**
A serve used primarily in doubles play.

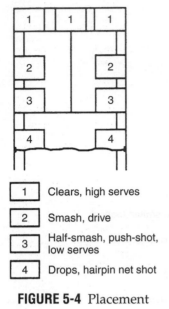

1	Clears, high serves
2	Smash, drive
3	Half-smash, push-shot, low serves
4	Drops, hairpin net shot

FIGURE 5-4 Placement areas.

the high, deep serve will take all the strength and power available to get the shuttle high enough and deep enough to be considered successful. The latter has much the same flight as the clear because it is hit to a point high above the backcourt and when it loses speed it turns and falls straight down. If the shuttle falls straight down on the back boundary line, your opponent must be that far back in the court to return it. If it is too flat and too low, the receiver will intercept it before it ever gets to the backcourt.

Conversely, the shuttle hit with a low serve has a flat arc as it just skims over the net and into the court near the short service line.

The low serve in doubles requires the same grip and foot position. However, the backswing is shortened, the shuttle contacted as near waist level as possible and perhaps slightly more to the right. The shuttle is guided over the net without wrist motion. A great deal less shoulder and arm power will be needed to hit the short distance and low trajectory required for the low serve.

Because the serve is played underhand and therefore must be hit upward, it is considered a defensive stroke. Consequently, to score, the server must eventually turn defense into attack. The receiver cannot score a point; therefore, the receiver's objective is to stay on the attack and win the opportunity to serve, making it possible then to score. This peculiarity of badminton—having to score from a beginning defensive position—prolongs a game even though no points are recorded.

UNDERHAND CLEAR

Many of the same stroke production fundamentals of the high, deep, singles serve—the grip, the wrist and arm power, and the follow-through—can be applied to the underhand clear. When stroking this clear, swing the racket down from the ready position, under the shuttle for contact and up, following through in the intended direction of the shuttle. Except if it originates near the net, the flight pattern the shuttle makes mimics the high, deep serve. Note figure 5-1.

Just as with the overhead defensive clear (described later), use the underhand clear to gain time to recover the center position and to force your opponent to the backcourt. The underhand clear's values are many in both singles and doubles. For example, if a drop is not particularly good and does not fall close to the net, a large choice of shots is available. Near-perfect drops necessitate a return with an underhand clear, in which case this stroke becomes indispensable. The only alternative to using the underhand clear is the hairpin net shot described later in this chapter.

UNDERHAND DROP

The underhand drop described here is played from an area between midcourt and the short service line to the opponent's side of the net as near to the net as possible. It has specific use both in singles and doubles (figure 5-1). Closely related, and yet different in its use, is the drop played from closer to the net.

The fundamentals of stroking and the characteristics of the underhand drop are almost identical with those of the low serve. A slow, controlled shot, the drop has its limitations for this reason: if you hit the shuttle from the baseline at a slow pace, your opponent has time to pounce on it at the net. Unless the underhand drop is disguised, ineffective returns result. Although rarely played successfully from the baseline, this stroke's values are exceptional in doubles and mixed doubles when played from midcourt. In doubles, the drop is used to run the net player from side to side or to draw a player up when both players are back. In singles, it can be a superb return of a smash. Directed crosscourt away from the smasher, the drop forces the opponent to recover quickly and to run the long distance.

OVERHEAD STROKES

THE CLEAR

The overhead stroke is similar to the motion of throwing a baseball. The most basic badminton shot hit with this stroke is the clear—a high shot deep to the back of the opponent's court. The **high clear** is a defensive shot, used to recover or gain time. A variation, the **attacking clear,** is an effective offensive shot (figure 5-5).

▶ Procedure (see figures 5-6 and 5-7)

1. Take the proper forehand grip, watch the approaching shuttle, and use the prescribed footwork. Move yourself to a place where you are in correct relationship to the shuttle.
2. As you are moving to this position behind the shuttle, swing your racket and arm back behind your head and shoulders. This will require pivoting at your waist and turning your shoulders sideways to the net. This position is

▶ **High Clear and Attacking Clear**
The high clear is a defensive shot, used to recover or gain time. A variation, the attacking clear, is an effective offensive shot.

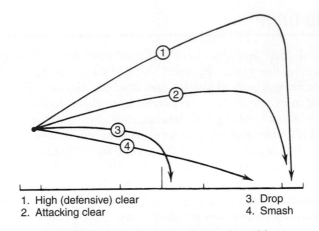

1. High (defensive) clear
2. Attacking clear
3. Drop
4. Smash

FIGURE 5-5 Flight patterns produced by overhead strokes.

FIGURE 5-6 Overhead clear.

fundamentally the same as that taken by a baseball outfielder making an over-arm throw to home plate. In badminton the racket, instead of the ball, is in your hand, but it is literally thrown at the shuttle in the identical fashion.

3. Rotate your forearm and wrist inward as you move the racket from behind your head. This rotation, called **pronation,** continues through the entire stroke.

Contacting the shuttle too late   Standing flat to the net

FIGURE 5-7 Mistakes most commonly made with the overhead clear.

4. Incorrectly allowing your arm to drop and bend when stroking results in loss of power. With full power, contact the shuttle with your arm fully extended and ahead of your body.
5. Rotate your trunk forward during this stroke to gain power.
6. Your ideal position is behind and in line with the shuttle.
7. Always hit the shuttle as soon as possible so that your opponent will not have time to get your shots.
8. Meet the shuttle with a flat racket without any cutting or slicing motion. Cutting gives control but takes away power.

   Here are some additional suggestions for achieving a successful clear.

1. The shuttlecock is difficult to slice because of its feathers and does not react as a spinning ball; therefore, it is essential to learn how to exert power.
2. The contact of the racket and shuttle must be explosive to get distance because there is little weight on the racket.
3. The angle of the racket face upon contact is the final determining factor as to the direction the shuttle will take.

▶ **Pronation**

The inward turning of the wrist and forearm used in all powerful overhead forehand strokes.

4. Be sure to move your weight into the shot as the stroke is made.
5. Note the flight pattern of the clear in figure 5-5. The shuttle is hit high enough so that at a certain point, almost above the back boundary line, it loses speed and turns and falls straight down. A shuttle falling at right angles to the floor is difficult to play. It is important to hit the shuttle with depth because your opponent will be unable to smash a clear effectively from the back boundary line.

▶ High Clear Strategy

The high or defensive clear is used primarily to gain time for the player to return to the center position in the court. One of the most valuable benefits of this shot is derived from its use in combinations with the drop to run your opponent to all four corners of the court.

As can be seen in figure 5-5, depth and height of the shuttlecock are extremely important on the defensive clear to force your opponent as far into the backcourt as possible.

Your next shot, a drop just over the net, would become effective in this game of maneuvering for openings and spaces. It might also force your opponent to hit a short return that could be smashed. It takes a strong player to clear from one baseline to the opposite one and an extraordinarily strong player to high clear crosscourt to the diagonal corner. Unless a shuttle that flies very fast is used, it is unlikely that the average player would be able to accomplish this difficult feat. Consequently, in singles, the player who hits a high deep defensive clear gains control of the rally and should eventually win that point.

Analyzing a match played by contestants of equal skill demonstrates that the player who consistently has good length always wins. When playing, if you find you do not have time to reach the shots and each point is a struggle, then check the length of your clears. Your opponent will seldom hit a winning shot or putaway if your clear is deep enough. Also, clears that are too low and too short are cut off before they reach the backcourt.

▶ The Attacking Clear

After learning the basic high deep clear, you can develop the attacking clear, a modification. Its use should not be confused with that of the defensive clear, or else disaster will result.

1. The trajectory of the attacking clear is not as high, but the shot is faster. There is a different arc to the flight pattern, as can be seen in figure 5-5.
2. The attacking clear can be used more successfully when the opponent is out of center position because the arc is low.
3. Often the attacking clear is best used following a good drop to the forehand corner. The clear can then be hit quickly to the backhand corner while your opponent is recovering from the net.
4. Once the clear gets behind the opponent on the backhand, the return is more likely to be in the forecourt. When an opponent's return is forced to be short, the point should be yours! A defensive clear incorrectly used in this situation would

give the opponent time to move back and hit overhead, and your advantage would be lost.

The only difference in the production of these two types of clears is that the attacking clear has a flatter arc; therefore, stroke it with less upward angle. It also requires more power, because without the upward angle, it would not travel far enough.

THE OVERHEAD DROP (SEE FIGURES 5-8 AND 5-9)

The overhead drop is a slow shot that drops just over the net in the opponent's forecourt.

▶ **Procedure**

1. Use exactly the same grip, footwork, body position, and backswing described for the overhead clear. Your intention should be to suggest that a clear is forthcoming.
2. The difference is wrist speed. There is less wrist rotation, and the shuttle is stroked with greater control rather than "patted."
3. Contact the shuttle farther ahead of your body to direct it downward.
4. The downward movement of your arm coupled with completion of your wrist action brings the shuttle down. Tilt the face of the racket downward at the angle you wish the shuttle to take.

FIGURE 5-8 Overhead drop.

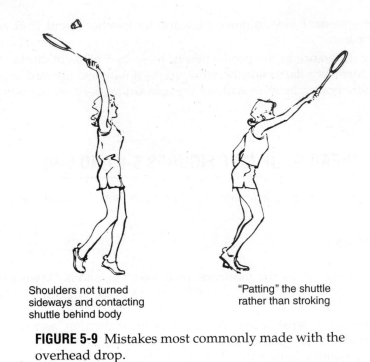

Shoulders not turned
sideways and contacting
shuttle behind body

"Patting" the shuttle
rather than stroking

FIGURE 5-9 Mistakes most commonly made with the
overhead drop.

5. Rotate your shoulder and trunk forward and move your weight into the shot
(figure 5-8).

▶ Advantages of the Drop

1. The drop is invaluable because it enables you to use the front corners of the
court. No other type of shot goes to the two front corners near the net.
2. The smash and drive are placed midcourt or deeper as shown in figures 5-5
and 5-13. Always place the drop in the forecourt. The drop, whether overhead,
underhand, or hit from the side, can be played from any place on the court.

▶ Strategy for the Drop

1. A major part of singles strategy lies in using the overhead drop in combination
with clears. For example, if clears are used repeatedly, a player tends to move
the basic position toward the rear of the court to cover the deep shots. This
position makes the drop doubly effective.
2. Singles becomes a game of up and back and up and back again until a weak
return is forced and a smash finishes the rally.
3. A midcourt shot, one halfway between the net and back boundary line, is not as
useful in singles as in doubles, because this shot does not move the opponent
out of center. Consequently, keep the shuttle as far from the center of the court
as possible with clears and drops.

4. Deception is the most outstanding characteristic of a good drop. If the drop is deceptive enough it can be an outright winner even though it might have been planned as a lead-up shot.
5. If your opponent is halfway to the net or at the net before your shot reaches the net, then your deception has not been sufficient and you have probably lost the exchange.
6. As you become more skilled with the drop, experiment by hitting it fast or slow and with more or less arc. Try slicing the shuttle slightly to slow it down and change its direction. This will add to the deception of the shot.
7. The least attractive characteristic of the drop is its slow flight. Anything moving slowly unfortunately gives your opponent what you don't want her or him to have—time. The drop, however, contributes to the essence of the game—measuring time and selecting shots in relation to your own and your opponent's position on the court.

THE SMASH (SEE FIGURES 5-10 AND 5-11)

The smash is a powerful overhead shot used to "put away" any shuttle above the height of the net.

1. In the interest of deception, the smash should be masked as a clear or a drop. Use the same grip, footwork, body position, backswing, and contact point as

FIGURE 5-10 Smash.

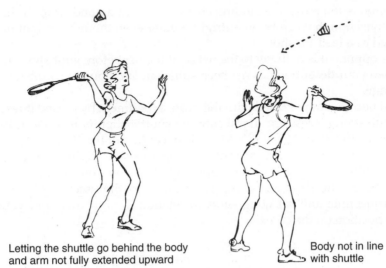

Letting the shuttle go behind the body
and arm not fully extended upward

Body not in line
with shuttle

FIGURE 5-11 Mistakes most commonly made with the smash.

with the clear and the drop, and your opponent will not anticipate your return.

2. The smash differs from the clear and the drop in that it can be hit only with an overhead stroke; a clear and a drop can come from either an overhead or underhand stroke.

3. Be sure you move to a position behind the shuttle as quickly as possible.

4. Take care to have a proper body position, because balance must be perfect to achieve maximum power from your shoulders, arms, and wrist. Your left shoulder must be turned to the net and your right shoulder back and ready to strike with force. See figure 5-11.

5. Cock your arm and wrist behind your body ready to unleash all available power. The racket head may be moving at a terrific rate as it goes out to meet the shuttle. The handle must be gripped firmly at the instant of contact.

6. Contact the shuttle at the highest comfortable point. The follow-through is down and in line with the flight of the shuttle.

7. Hit the overhead smash with as much power as that needed for the high deep clear. To get such power, rotate the wrist and forearm fully and rapidly and use perfect timing.

8. Rotate your trunk and shoulders forward and throw your weight into the shot. When you are first learning to smash, however, try to get your timing and downward angle correct before attempting to get excessive speed. Timing is thrown off if too much arm and body effort are involved in the stroke; let a swiftly rotating racket do the work.

9. The racket face must be angled downward at contact point to make the shuttle travel sharply downward.
10. The farther away you are from the net, the less angle and speed the smash can carry.

▶ Strategy

Two reasons for using a smash:

1. It has more downward angle and speed than any other stroke, making it the main point-winning shot. If the pattern of play has developed as planned, your final shot of the rally will be an overhead smash.
2. If the smash is returned, the return will be an upward, or defensive, stroke because of the angle of your smash.

In both situations, the smash is an invaluable weapon. There is, however, a reason for avoiding indiscriminate use of the smash, namely, the effort needed to smash leaves your body off balance, and therefore it takes longer to recover your position than with other types of shots. Thus, your judgment as to when to smash rather than to clear or to drop is important. Many factors related to you and to your opponent will enter into this decision.

Examine figures 5-6, 5-8, and 5-10 to see the characteristics that are alike in making the various shots. The position of the feet and the body is the same for all overhead shots. The stroke pattern—backswing, forward swing, and follow-through—should also be almost identical for the overhead strokes in order to employ the deception necessary to make the shots effective. What, then, determines whether an overhead shot is to be a clear, a drop, or a smash?

The answer lies in the speed of the wrist, the degree of wrist action used, and the angle of the face of the racket at the moment of contact with the shuttle. On all badminton shots, cock the wrist back ready for the action that comes within the larger action of the shoulder and arm swing. Wrist power alone is not sufficient to propel the shuttle from one end of the court to the other; it necessitates arm power and shoulder rotation in addition to exact timing of the wrist snap as the weight moves forward. A player who intends to smash and put the shuttle "away" may leap off the ground for better angle and possible added power. In this case, deception can also be used to enhance the stroke because a clear and drop can be hit from the jump position.

▶ The Half-Paced Smash

The half-paced smash, popularly called "half-smash," is a smash with less speed. All elements of stroke production related to the smash apply to the half-smash. Keep the following points in mind:

1. The half-smash is played by contacting the shuttle with an extended arm diagonally above the head to obtain a steep angle downward.

2. To cut or slice the half-smash diminishes its speed and makes the shuttle fall close to the net at a sharper angle.
3. If the shuttle gets behind the player, the racket will be facing upward at contact point, the flight of the shuttle will be upward, and the shot will be a defensive one, in all probability a clear. It is important, therefore, that the shuttle be contacted well ahead of the body.
4. Caution: A smash hit with a bent arm results in loss of power and angle. The smash is then known as a "flat" smash, a highly undesirable shot.

The half-smash has as many values as the full, powerful smash, but is of a different nature. The half-smash can be played with less effort. Moreover, it can be played from deeper in the court because recovery of balance does not present a problem. Moving to cover the net return after the half-smash can be accomplished with ease. By contrast, a full smash from the backcourt leaves the front corners vulnerable. The use of the half-smash therefore is less risky. It is valuable, too, because of its sharply angled downward direction. By hitting downward, the attack is gained by forcing the opponent to stroke upward. Few points are won outright from an underhand stroke. The ones that are can be attributed to outright deception or to outpositioning the opponent.

▶ Angle of the Racket Face

The direction of the shuttle's flight in all overhead shots is determined by the **angle of the racket** face. Bringing the wrist and racket head through too soon causes an extreme downward angle to the shuttle, often resulting in a netted shot. Conversely, failure to bring the wrist and racket head through soon enough causes an extreme upward angle (figure 5-12).

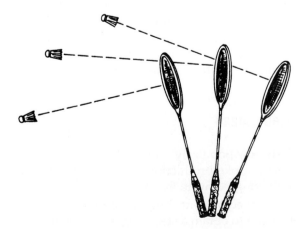

FIGURE 5-12 Angle of racket face.

SIDEARM STROKES

THE DRIVE

The drive is produced by a flat sidearm stroke played on the forehand or backhand. See figure 5-13 for flights of sidearm strokes.

▶ Forehand Drive (see figures 5-14 and 5-15)

The forehand drive is played on the right side of the body and is similar to the baseball sidearm throw (figure 5-14).

1. Take a forehand grip, turn your body until your left shoulder is to the net, and turn your shoulders to allow your arm to take the backswing (figure 5-15).

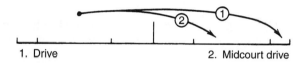

1. Drive   2. Midcourt drive

FIGURE 5-13 Flight patterns produced by sidearm strokes.

FIGURE 5-14 Forehand drive.

▶ Angle of the Racket Face
This determines the direction of the shuttle's flight in all overhead shots.

Shoulders not turned sideways

Shuttle contacted too late

FIGURE 5-15 Mistakes most commonly made with the forehand drive.

2. Place the head of the racket between your shoulder blades. To start the backswing, bend your elbow and cock your wrist backward in preparation for a powerful swing.
3. Watch the shuttle closely with the idea of contacting it diagonally ahead between shoulder and waist height (figure 5-15).
4. As your arm and racket swing forward, your body weight should transfer from your right foot to your left foot. Rotate your forearm and wrist inward during the stroke.
5. Contact the shuttle with a flat racket and well away from you so that your swing is not restricted.
6. Swing the racket on through in the direction of the flight of the shuttle. The speed of your swing compels the racket to complete its follow-through past the left shoulder. The racket has practically made a 360° circle. The action of the swing, particularly in the contact area, is explosive.
7. On many occasions, the forehand drive is played with the *right* foot extended toward the sideline. This allows for a farther reach without getting too far from the center position.

▶ **Backhand Drive (see figures 5-16 and 5-17)**

The backhand drive employs the same basic principles as the forehand drive with two or three exceptions (figure 5-16):
1. The grip is changed to the backhand grip; make sure that your thumb is flat on the handle. Now, rotate your forearm and wrist outward.
2. Elbow rotation is important in this and all other strokes. On the backswing your elbow is bent, your right hand is at your left shoulder, and your elbow is pointing at the oncoming shuttle (figure 5-17).

FIGURE 5-16 Backhand drive.

Elbow not pointing at shuttle

Contacting the shuttle too late

FIGURE 5-17 Mistakes most commonly made with the backhand drive.

3. Your weight shifts, your shoulders turn, your arm starts swinging forward with your elbow leading, and then the head of the racket whips over for the contact and follow-through (figure 5-17).

▶ Playing the Drives

Long, deep, fast drives and slower-paced midcourt drives can be played from either side of the body. Drives can be played like other shots, from one sideline diagonally across the court to the other sideline (crosscourt) or they can be played parallel to the sideline (down-the-line). The flight pattern of the drive is parallel to the floor and the shuttle just skims the net (figure 5-13). The drive is played anywhere from midcourt to backcourt and is driven to your opponent's deep court or midcourt depending on his or her location in the court.

The higher you can contact the shuttle on the drive, the less you will have to hit up. For example, if you hit the shuttle from below knee level it will have to go up to get over the net and will continue to rise as it carries on to midcourt.

If the shuttle rises to net level and then turns toward the floor because speed is lost, you have mistakenly hit a drop. Any shot higher than net level can be smashed and therein lies the danger of the hard-hit drive played from a low contact point. A drive less powerful (midcourt) may be of value if your opponent is not pulled out of position. The shuttle's arc will reach its peak at the net and descend from there on to midcourt. It therefore cannot be smashed.

Try never to provide your opponent with a setup for a smash.

Use the fast drive when an opponent is out of position and you wish to get the shuttle behind her or him to the backcourt. Perhaps you hit a well-placed drop to the forehand. The deep backhand corner is now briefly open. If your opponent returns your drop to your forehand, your problem is simple. If the shot is played down-the-line to your backhand, your problem is not so simple. You must get the shuttle there quickly before your opponent gains the center of the court or the shot will be blocked off for a winner while you are still recovering from the execution of your stroke. It takes more time to recover body balance and center position from hard-hit power shots than from drops, midcourt drives, or net shots.

If the two drives are used correctly and intelligently, they can be valuable attacking weapons. Used badly, they can cause disaster.

▶ Angle of the Racket Face

The direction of the shuttle's flight is determined by the angle of the racket face. It will require a great deal of practice to learn to control the moment of impact of the racket head and the shuttle to direct shots down-the-line or crosscourt.

NET PLAY

DESCRIPTION

Net play is a general term encompassing those shots played from the area around the short service line to the net (figure 5-18). Net play, which includes the hairpin net shot described in this chapter as well as the push shot and the net smash described in chapter 7, is important because the front of the court has to be defended.

The forehand grip is satisfactory for net play but the backhand grip must be adjusted slightly:

1. The side of the thumb is placed up the back bevel of the racket, which may cause a slight turning of the hand toward the forehand grip.
2. The wrist is used differently for net shots, that is, with little relationship to the shoulders and body. The grip adjustment allows such wrist action. Conversely, this grip could not be used successfully to perform a clear from the backhand corner.

FIGURE 5-18 Net play.

On both forehand and backhand strokes, spread the fingers and hold the racket almost loosely. This should give more "touch." To get even more control, hold the racket slightly up from the end. This shortening of the grip gives less power (not needed at net) and less reach. You must decide, therefore, what you wish to gain (control) and what you wish to sacrifice (reach).

The feet, body, and upper arm are used for reaching rather than for stroke production; the actual strokes are done with the forearm, wrist, and hand. The racket meets the shuttle with a flat face. The wrist action may be smooth and controlled or it may be quick, depending on the type of net shot you are attempting. The explosive power so essential for clears and smashes is not needed in the forecourt.

The follow-through should be in the direction in which you wish the shuttle to travel. Guide it and go with it. At times, the follow-through must be abbreviated to avoid hitting the net. According to the rules, a player may not hit the net while the shuttle is in play. It is in play until it hits the net or floor.

Your court position for net play in singles and doubles should be such that your extended arm and racket can just touch the net. This distance from the net will permit unrestricted movement of your arm. In doubles it will also enable you to cover more midcourt shots.

In net play take fast, small steps, which allow you to turn and move quickly in any direction. The right foot should be forward on all net shots.

The most difficult shots to play at net are those falling perpendicular to the floor rather than diagonally. Diagonally dropping shuttles arrive farther back in the court; perpendicular falling shuttles, at their best, touch or almost touch the net as they fall toward the floor. These are difficult to play, and because they cannot be directed forward, only upward, they are called hairpin drops. Your opponent, sensing this, is alert to smash as soon as the shuttle comes up and over the net.

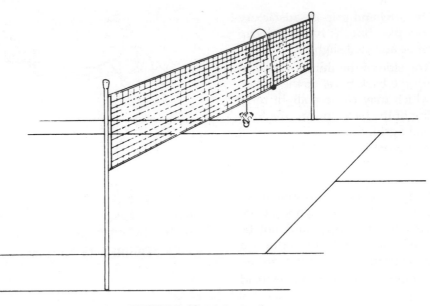

FIGURE 5-19 Hairpin drop.

HAIRPIN DROP

The **hairpin drop** gets its name from the flight pattern of the shuttle (figure 5-19). Played from one side of the net to the other, it should fall perpendicular to the floor and close to the net on the opponent's side. This shot travels the least distance of any badminton shot; consequently, little stroke is needed. The shuttle played at net level may be tapped or blocked back. Played well below net level, it will have to be stroked with great care up and over the net. Some championship players stroke the shuttle with a slicing action, which gives the shuttle less speed and a spinning motion that is difficult to return. The perfect hairpin drop results in the shuttle's crawling up and over the net and trickling down the other side.

A FINAL WORD ON STROKES AND SHOTS

With all strokes, the learning process is slow and gradual while you are acquiring increased accuracy, depth, and speed. As you continue to play and practice, the shuttle will travel more often in the direction in which you aim it. You will attain more power in clears and smashes and (desirably) less speed in drops. To help you stroke your shots effectively and with care, you must correctly execute basic positions and footwork. The entire process, then, is one of smooth coordination. Chapter 9 contains a series of drills that offer repetitive practice for all the shots in this chapter.

In every sport involving eye-hand contact, there is one fundamental principle that cannot be overemphasized. In the case of golf or tennis it is "keep your eye on the ball." In badminton it is "keep your eye on the shuttlecock." If you do not watch the shuttlecock, one of the following mistakes will occur:

1. You will miss the shuttlecock entirely.
2. You will hit the feathers of the shuttlecock.
3. You will not hit the shuttle in the center of the racket, often causing an inaccurate shot.

SUMMARY

- The underhand, overhead, and sidearm strokes are the basic strokes in badminton. Consult each stroke's section in this chapter, as each gives a detailed account.
- Net play is a general term encompassing those shots played from the area around the short service line to the net. This is important because the front of the court has to be defended.

▶ **Hairpin Drop**

A shot made from below and close to the net with the shuttle rising, just clearing the net, and then dropping sharply down the other side. The shuttle's flight approximates the shape of a hairpin.

Assessment 5-1

Name   Section   Date

1. In most racket sports the serve is considered an attacking stroke. Why is this not the case in badminton? The shuttle should drop to the racket when executing a high serve. What may result if, instead, the racket is brought up to the shuttle?
2. Describe ways to increase power on the high clear.
3. Why is it important for the high clear to fall near the back boundary line?
4. Is it desirable to deceive your opponent as to whether you intend to make a drop, clear, or smash? How can this be done?
5. How can you determine your best court position for net play? What is the role of the feet, body, and upper arm when executing a net shot?

CHAPTER 6

STRATEGIES AND TACTICS

After reading this chapter, you should know the fundamental strategies and tactics for the competitive forms of badminton:

- Singles.
- Doubles.
- Mixed doubles.

KEY TERMS

While reading this chapter, you will become familiar with the following terms:

▶ Offense

▶ Defense

▶ Angle of Return

▶ Crosscourt Shots

▶ Return of Serve

▶ Side-by-Side Formation

▶ Up-and-Back Formation

▶ Rotation

Certain strategies and tactics apply to all forms of badminton. Strategies are "plans made for accomplishing an end"; tactics are "skillful devices" for carrying out these ends. Winning badminton is a question of playing basic fundamentals better than your opponent and understanding and applying strategic principles.

OFFENSE AND DEFENSE

In **offensive** play, shots are directed downward. They are point-winning shots such as smashes, half-smashes, drops, and low serves. Winning a point from an overhead position requires speed, sharp angles, and accurate direction. Winning a point from an underhand stroke has to be accomplished through deception or superior court positioning.

In **defensive** play, shots are directed upward. These shots include clears, underhand drops, and high serves. Drives, being shots with a horizontal trajectory, can be offensive or defensive, depending on their angle of return and on the position of the opponent(s). Offensive and defensive positions may change during the course of a rally, depending on how well a stroke is executed and selected for use at the proper time. For example, if you return a smash with an underhand hairpin drop properly angled away from the smasher and the shot falls close to the net, the smasher is forced to hit up (defensive). If, however, the smash had been returned with an underhand clear or weak net shot, the offensive would have remained with the smasher.

Offensive players take chances and strive for outright winners, whereas defensive players are content to "play it safe" and wait for the opponent to err.

ANGLE OF RETURN

The **angle of return** is as important in badminton as it is in tennis and other racket games. It is the angle the returned shuttle takes in relation to the court boundaries. It does not refer to upward or downward angle.

▶ **Offense**
State of being on the attack; a style of play consisting mainly of attacking clears, fast drops, and smashes.

▶ **Defense**
State of being under attack by the oppo-

nent; a style of play consisting mainly of slow drops and high clears.

▶ **Angle of Return**
The angle the returned shuttle takes in relation to the court boundaries.

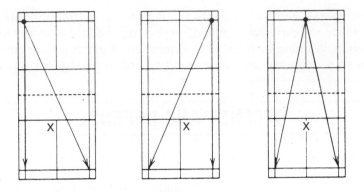

FIGURE 6-1 Angles of return and base position.

To avoid being trapped by angle of return, position yourself on the court where the greater percentages of returns are likely to come. Occasionally you can neglect a portion of the court, a situation you strive for. This is a form of intelligent anticipation. The best plan is to maintain your position in the center of the angle of possible returns and then be alert to the odd shot (figure 6-1).

Examples:

1. A high clear to your opponent's deep forehand or backhand corner can rarely be returned crosscourt high and deep to your diagonal corner because of the long distance. It could be returned with a flat, fast clear toward that corner, but you will be in the center blocking it before it reaches the intended spot.
2. A shot played to the center of the opponent's court will place the center of the angle of return on the center line.

CROSSCOURT SHOTS

Crosscourting and angle of return are closely related. **Crosscourt shots** travel a longer distance across the court and take more time to reach the intended spot than down-the-line shots. Down-the-line shots travel a shorter distance and are more logical, but more obvious. For example, if you play the shuttle to your opponent's forehand side, anticipate the straight return to your backhand side. Your opponent can crosscourt to your forehand side, but the longer distance gives you more time to reach it.

Crosscourt when you are on balance and are able to return to center quickly and/or when the opponent has overanticipated.

1. A crosscourt shot of any kind played from forehand to forehand leaves the vulnerable backhand exposed.
2. Most of the time, move about a foot to the side of the court to which you have directed the shuttle.

3. Move a step forward if your shot has forced your opponent to the baseline. He or she may be unable to get sufficient depth from your good length.

Try to trap your opponent into overanticipating certain shots by playing cross-court or down-the-line shots in a specific pattern. Then play the odd shot for a winner or to draw the opponent away from a particular area. Many players leave the forehand side open and vulnerable in an effort to cover up a weak backhand.

Have a preconceived idea of how much you intend to use crosscourt shots and how to play each opponent. As the game progresses, both players will be trying various plans in hopes of achieving a successful one.

RECEIVING SERVE

READY POSITION

Your ready position for return of serve for singles and doubles is a modification of the ready position during a rally.

1. Place your feet comfortably apart with your left foot ahead of the right in a diagonal stance, rather than with your feet side by side and parallel. This enables you to have an immediate push forward or backward depending on whether it is a low or high deep serve.
2. It is imperative to be prepared to move forward to smash a poor low serve or to move backward before the high serve gets behind you. Therefore, after taking your position to receive serve, keep your feet stationary until the server contacts the shuttle.

RECEIVING

It is important to anticipate the usual direction of the serves and to adjust your position accordingly, shifting your weight in that direction to get a faster start.

1. Do not overanticipate. If you do, the server is given the opportunity to surprise you with a change in direction or depth. Take care to keep your percentages in the proper balance.
2. Note in figure 6-2 that the receiver in the right service court is standing closer to the center line than to the sideline to protect his or her backhand side. The

▶ **Crosscourt Shots**

A shot that travels a longer distance across the court and takes more time to reach the intended spot than down-the-line shots.

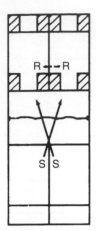

FIGURE 6-2
Receiving
serve in
singles.

receiver in the left service court moves toward the backhand side for the same purpose.

3. In both cases the receiver is closer to the short service line than to the long service line. This position enables the receiver to attack (hit down) the low serve if it appears but requires more time to move back for the high deep serve.

▶ **Common Faults in Receiving Serve**

1. Standing too deep in the court, resulting in a defensive (hitting up) return of the low serve.
2. Moving back too slowly, letting the shuttle get behind you.

Whether you are playing singles or doubles, the general rule is to change your position if you are encountering difficulties. Find the place in the court and the position that best suits you and best defies your opponent's plans.

SINGLES STRATEGY

Singles can be described as a "running" game because it requires excellent physical condition to cover the seventeen-by-twenty-two foot area. Singles can be a difficult game for some players because it can expose weaknesses that might otherwise be covered up by a partner in doubles play. In general, singles offers the greatest challenge to individual skill and stamina.

The most effective shots in singles play are the high deep serve, overhead clear (both high and attacking), drop, half-smash, underhand clear, and hairpin drop. Shots used less frequently are the low serve, drive serve, drive, push shot, and the full smash.

SERVES

The high deep serve moves the opponent out of center to the back boundary line and thus opens up the front of the court. The low serve used as a change of pace is a method of gaining the offensive because the shuttle may descend as it reaches the top of the net. Therefore, it usually cannot be smashed downward.

▶ **Return of Serve**

A clear to the opposite baseline is the best and safest return of a deep high serve. If the high serve is short you can hit a drop, smash, half-smash, or attacking clear. The offensive can thus be gained with an attacking shot. Choose the shot that you can execute effectively and deceptively.

As in the **return of serve,** short clears during the rally are disastrous. They can be dealt with more easily and with more variety than shots that fall perpendicularly on the back boundary line.

ATTACK

To attack effectively, remember the following:
1. Force your opponent to play a backhand from deep court.
2. Force your opponent to hit short by using good depth.
3. Hit to the forehand corner to open up the backhand side.
4. Meet the shuttle as soon as possible to give your opponent less time.
5. Be deceptive—but it is difficult to be deceptive unless you have plenty of time and are not struggling to reach the shuttle.

DEFENSE

When the opportunity arises for your opponent to play a smash or a drop you must defend as well as possible. Return the shuttle close to the net or the baseline as midcourt shots have little value here. Try to use your opponent's speed or angle to your advantage by blocking or guiding the shuttle just over the net with a hairpin drop. Direct the shuttle to the farthest distance from the attacker.

For example, if your opponent smashes or drops from the deep forehand corner, then you should hit a hairpin drop to the front backhand corner. If your opponent anticipates the net shot and comes racing in toward the net, flick a flat clear to the backhand corner. Next time go ahead and play the net shot. Alternate your pattern or, better yet, make your pattern random, so your opponent doesn't know what return to expect or where to expect it.

TYPES OF SINGLES PLAY

1. The fast and quick game includes such shots as the low serve, drive serve, flat or attacking clear, drive, and smash.
2. The slower and more deliberate game includes the high serve, high clear, drop, and half-smash.

Many players are adept at both fashions of play, and the use of a particular one depends on the opponent and the situation.

▶ **Return of Serve**
In singles, it is best to clear to the opposite baseline.

DOUBLES STRATEGY

Doubles play requires quick racket skill, wit, and cleverness. It is exciting, extremely fast, and demands excellent teamwork. It also requires less stamina than singles and is a game in which weaknesses can be disguised.

The most effective doubles serves include the low serve and flick serve. The most useful doubles shots are the drive, half-smash, smash, and various net returns. This is because a team that hits up often is less likely to win. A team that disciplines itself to hit down consistently can often beat a more physically talented team that hits up with abandon.

Through various maneuvers by the two partners, a player may not have to use his or her less adequate strokes. Instead, both players combine their best assets. Partners unequal in ability can work out a combination that is unusually stable and effective.

Four players, all of different skill levels, can combine and have great fun playing.

SYSTEMS OF PLAY

The three systems of doubles play are:
- side-by-side (defensive)
- up-and-back (offensive)
- rotation (a combination of the two)

Men's and women's doubles teams use all three systems although most prefer rotation. Mixed doubles teams prefer the up-and-back formation.

▶ Side-by-Side or Defensive Formation

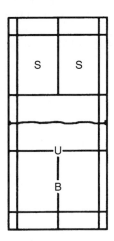

A team in a **side-by-side formation** (S and S) divides the court down the middle from net to back boundary line (figure 6-3). Each player covers half of the court, both front and back. The basic serving and receiving positions for the team playing side by side place each player in the middle of his or her half of the court.

These positions, alterable as the situation changes, are defensive positions. The down-the-middle shots, those directed between the two players, are usually played by the player on the left side because the center is that player's forehand side. A team with a left-handed player will discover some interesting advantages and disadvantages, requiring some decisions. It could be agreed that the stronger player is to play the middle shots regardless of either player's forehand side.

FIGURE 6-3
Side-by-side and up-and-back doubles formations.

The advantage of the sides system is that the area that each player is to defend is well-defined and there is little confusion about who is to cover which shots. This defensive side formation is the best system when you have been forced to hit the shuttle upward, thus giving your opponents the opportunity to smash. With both players back from the net, they have more time to defend against the smash and to cover the areas (midcourt and backcourt) where a smash can be directed.

The disadvantage of the system is that the opposite team can play all the shots to one side, up and back, and tire one player. If one player is weaker than the other, the opponents will naturally launch their attack on that player.

▶ Up-and-Back or Offensive Formation

In this system the court is divided in such a way that one player (U) plays the forecourt and the other player (B) plays the backcourt (figure 6-3). Note the serving (S) and receiving (R) positions for this formation in figure 6-4. The dividing line is about midcourt, depending upon the agreement made by the two partners (P).

The advantage of the **up-and-back formation** lies in that there is always a player at the net to "put away" any loose returns. This keeps the pressure on the opponents.

For example, as soon as one player can smash or drop from the backcourt, his or her partner moves forward to the net position to cut off any weak returns. Crosscourt shots can be more easily blocked with a player at the net. In addition, this formation makes it easier to protect weaknesses, as players can cover the part of the court to which their game is best suited.

The disadvantage of the up-and-back system is that the midcourt area along the sidelines is vulnerable. The half-court shot that is played just behind the net player and just in front of the backcourt

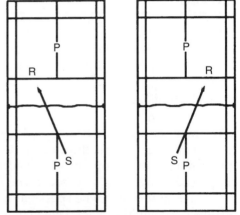

FIGURE 6-4 Up-and-back doubles formation serving to right and left courts.

▶ **Side-by-Side Formation**
A team divides the court down the middle from net to back boundary line.

▶ **Up-and-Back Formation**
A doubles formation, particularly predominant in mixed doubles.

player tends to cause confusion as to which player is to hit the shuttle. The resulting slight delay may prove disastrous.

▶ **Rotation**

The **rotation** system is a means of changing from up-and-back to side-by-side depending on whether a team is attacking or defending.

The attacking team will have to relinquish the up-and-back formation when either player is forced to hit the shuttle upward (defensive). The up-and-back formation is an inadequate defense against the smash because the player at net will not have time to defend, and his or her partner cannot protect the entire backcourt against a smash. The net player should backpedal quickly to either side, preferably the closer, and the partner adjusts accordingly. Therefore, when forced on defense, this team reverts to the side-by-side formation until it can regain the attack.

A team on defense can regain the attack by returning smashes with a well-placed halfcourt or drive. The player hitting such a shot should move to the net while the partner pulls around behind him or her, in the up-and-back position, to attack the next shot.

SERVES

Whatever the system used, the serve is important as it gives the opportunity to score. In doubles, the low serve is best and most often used. The flick and drive serves (see chapter 7) are also used effectively as alternatives.

▶ **Return of Serve**

Any high serve should be returned with an overhead drop or more preferably a smash. However, most of the time the receiver will be low served and has a choice of returning with a drop, drive, or halfcourt. The *drop* should be deceptive; low; and played straight, not crosscourt. The *drive* return is used most often and ideally has a flat trajectory, and when possible, it is directed to the backhand side although the direction should be varied when necessary. The *halfcourt* is the most difficult to execute as it has to be almost perfect or it backfires. It should fall behind the net player at a downward angle to force the back player to hit up.

OFFENSE

The primary object of the serve, return of serve, and succeeding shots is to force your opponents to hit up thereby giving your side the attack. When this objective is reached, the smash, the half-smash, and overhead drop come into play. The smash should win the point outright or force a weak return for the net person to "put away." When smashing, it is important to be on balance and for the smash to have a sharp downward angle. It should be played to the inside of the opponent who is straight ahead of you or directly down the middle. Crosscourt smash only for variety and to keep both opponents alert. The half-smash is extremely useful to change the pace, particularly after full paced smashes have been used. Overhead drops will take less effort and therefore they have their merits. Indiscriminate and nonpurposeful smashing is not intelligent. Mix the overhead drop, smash, and half-smash judiciously and the rewards will be obvious.

DEFENSE

Despite all efforts to keep the shuttle going down to maintain the offense, at times your opponents will force you to defend. How good or how bad your opponents are will determine the amount of time you spend defending your court! The smash and drop can be returned with a high deep clear or better yet with a flatter shot at head or shoulder level. The high deep clear keeps you on defense only with the hope of an error by the smasher. The half-court or drive return initiates the turn from defense to offense.

MIXED DOUBLES STRATEGY

The systems of doubles play described are used in men's doubles, women's doubles, and recreational doubles play involving men and women players, with the relative strengths of the players often determining the system and the positions chosen. On the other hand, mixed doubles is a particular event in tournament and club badminton. Traditionally, it is played by the man and woman in an up-and-back formation because, at this level of competition, the speed and the smashing power of the man usually exceeds those of the woman. With the up-and-back formation, it is impossible for the man to concentrate his attack on the opposing woman with any degree of success. A more well-balanced game results, superior to many games involving men and women.

The following strategies are written with this traditional mixed doubles formation in mind, but they also offer advice to regular doubles teams who elect the up-and-back formation exclusively.

See figures 6-5 and 6-6 for serving and receiving positions.

▶ **Rotation**
   Rotation of the side-by-side and up-and-
   back doubles formations.

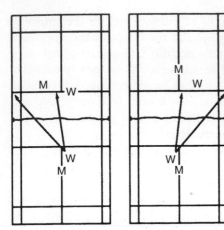

FIGURE 6-5 Mixed doubles formation—woman serving.

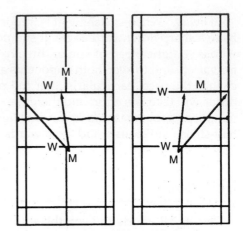

FIGURE 6-6 Mixed doubles formation—man serving.

DUTIES OF THE WOMAN (OR FRONT) PLAYER

1. Place shots in the front court and around the short service line.
2. Control the attack by directing the shuttle downward.
3. Use net and half-court shots to direct shuttle downward.
4. Smash any "loose" (high and short) shots.
5. Let clears, fast drives, and smashes pass by to be played by the partner.
6. Rarely move to the backcourt to play.

DUTIES OF THE MAN (OR BACK) PLAYER

1. Play shots behind and around the short service line.
2. Play half-court shots, drives, and smashes.
3. Play downward shots that will force a weak return for the partner to "put away."

USE OF THE LOW SERVE

1. Keep it low and controlled, usually to the inside corner (less angle).
2. Serve to the outside corner occasionally to keep the receiver off balance.
3. Flick serve to keep the receiver off balance and from constantly rushing the low serve.
4. Serve high to the player who is slow moving back or has limited strength overhead.

RETURN OF SERVE

1. The half-court shot is the safest and most used. It has moderate speed, falls behind the woman at a downward angle, forcing the man to hit up. Play the halfcourt straight rather than crosscourt most of the time.
2. The drop is best used when the woman is serving and should be placed in the alley farthest from her. A drop is risky on the man's serve as his partner is near the net in an attacking position.
3. The drive is pushed or punched faster than the halfcourt and deeper in the court. Sometimes a punch directly at the man cramps him and narrows his angle of return as well.

STRATEGY

1. Use the drop and halfcourt to keep the opposing woman guessing and off balance.
2. Use the halfcourt and drive against the opposing man. These shots are best and safest because they are not hit up and they are intended to force an upward return. An upward return invites a smash, and smashes win points.
3. Avoid lifting or hitting the shuttle up.

The rallies often generate into driving duels between two men with the better drive winning. If you concede that the opposing man is excellent at driving, then make more use of the halfcourt and perhaps the drop if the woman is less effective than her partner. It is important for the man to use good judgment when electing to crosscourt a drive by being cognizant of his center position.

SPECIAL DEFENSIVE POSITION

Occasions will arise when you will be forced to hit up and defend against a smash. Usually the woman should back up several feet and defend against the crosscourt smash. She should hold her racket in front of her face for protection as she watches the shuttle and attempts to play it. The man is then responsible for the down-the-line smash and for the drop played straight. This net area has now become vulnerable because the woman has backed out and to one side in an effort to return the crosscourt smash.

SUMMARY

- As in any sport, badminton requires offense and defense. In offensive play, the shots (e.g., smashes, half-smashes, and drops) are directed downward. In defensive play, the shots are directed upward.

- The angle of return is important in badminton. There are a few steps you can take to avoid being trapped by the angle of return.
- Singles can be considered a "running" game because it requires a player on each side of the net to cover his or her side of the court. Effective strategies for successful singles play include the high deep serve, the overhead clear, the half-smash, the underhand clear, and the hairpin drop return.
- Doubles may require less stamina than singles, but it demands excellent communication and teamwork. There are three systems of doubles play: side-by-side, up-and-back, and rotation. Whatever the formation, the most effective doubles shots include the drive, half-smash, smash, and various net returns.
- Partners do not enjoy each other if they feel they are not getting to play their own or best shots. The man should not play shots better played by the woman. The woman should hit shots that produce returns capitalizing on the man's strengths.

Assessment 6-1

Name   Section   Date

1. Which areas of the court are most vulnerable in the up-and-back formation? In the side-by-side formation? Please use this space to draw a court and display your answer.
2. Usually, the woman plays up in the mixed doubles game. Do you know when it is advisable for her to drop back a few feet?
3. In mixed doubles, the woman should let certain shots go past to be played by her partner. Can you name these shots?

CHAPTER 7

TECHNIQUES FOR
BETTER PLAYERS

OBJECTIVES

After reading this chapter, you should know the fundamental stroking techniques and strategies for advanced strokes and shots for:

- The forehand.
- The backhand.
- The serve.
- Net play.

KEY TERMS

While reading this chapter, you will become familiar with the following terms:

▶ Round-the-Head Stroke

▶ "Scissors" Action

▶ High Backhand Stroke

▶ Flick Serve

▶ Balk

▶ Drive Serve

▶ Backhand Serve

▶ "Holding" the Shuttle

Continued on p. 77.

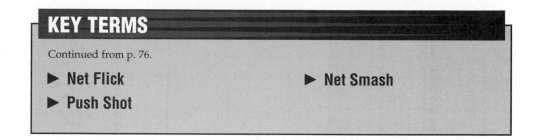

Continued from p. 76.

▶ **Net Flick**   ▶ **Net Smash**

▶ **Push Shot**

It is fun to experiment with additional strokes and shots to use in combination with the essential skills described in chapters 4 and 5. Descriptions of advanced techniques, such as the round-the-head and high backhand strokes, varieties of serves, forms of deception, and more advanced net play, will be found in this chapter. Many of these strokes are no more difficult to execute than the basic ones, but they consist of refinements and variations that are easier to learn once the basic strokes are mastered. Dwelling too soon on spectacular shots, at the expense of the standard ones used most of the time, tends to be discouraging and counterproductive.

Nevertheless, as you gain experience and perfect your basic strokes, you will want to add threat to your game. That your opponent must be alert to this possibility further assures the effectiveness of the basic strokes.

ADVANCED STROKES AND SHOTS

THE ROUND-THE-HEAD STROKE

The **round-the-head stroke** is an overhead forehand stroke, but it is unusual because the shuttle is contacted on the left or backhand side of the body. This stroke may be used to produce a clear, a drop, or a smash. The execution of this stroke is similar to that of the normal overhead forehand (see chapter 5 for instructions), but there are differences in footwork and in the path of the racket swing, described in the following section.

▶ **Round-the-Head Stroke**

An overhead forehand stroke played on the backhand side of the body. The contact point is usually above the opposite shoulder, and a clear, drop, or smash can result.

FIGURE 7-1 Round-the-head stroke.

▶ Procedure

1. The major difference from the normal overhead stroke is that the contact point is above your left shoulder, necessitating a reach to the left and a leaning of the body.
2. The stroke is played with your body facing the net and either with the weight on the left foot (figure 7-1) or with the body in the air (figure 7-2).
3. The right leg and body weight swing forward to the follow-through. If the stroke is taken with the body in the air, the legs execute a **"scissors" action** as the right leg swings forward and the left leg plants on the court after the shot to push back to center.

▶ Strategy

Many reasons exist for taking the shuttle with a round-the-head stroke rather than with a backhand stroke. First, more power and deception are usually possible on the round-the-head than on the backhand. This means you put more depth and speed on the shuttle, and hence produce a more effective shot. In addition, because your opponent will often be attacking your backhand corner, it is imperative that this area be protected at every opportunity. The round-the-head stroke meets this need. For example, if you can anticipate an attacking clear or drive serve to the backhand, intercept the shuttle in front of your body and hit it more quickly with a round-the-head shot.

The results of this stroke are not always favorable, however, as your feet and body have to be moved to the left side of the court and a large portion of your forehand side of the court is left open. Advantages gained by the round-the-head, such as a stronger shot, will have to be weighed against the disadvantages. The strength of your backhand and your speed of foot will be determining factors

FIGURE 7-2 Round-the-head stroke.

in selecting the round-the-head instead of the backhand. The ideal player will be able to play the high backhand stroke as well as the round-the-head.

THE HIGH BACKHAND STROKE

Many players believe that the **high backhand stroke,** particularly one used to produce a clear shot from deep court, is the most difficult stroke in badminton. This is not necessarily the case, especially given the light rackets available. If you follow the procedures listed, you will be able to hit clears, drops, and even smashes with the high backhand. The most important thing to remember is that, contrary to all other shots, the high backhand is best hit with the shuttle slightly behind your body and with your back partly turned toward the net (figure 7-3).

▶ **"Scissors" Action**
In a round-the-head stroke, the player's legs execute a "scissors" motion as the right leg swings forward and the left leg plants on the court after the shot to push back to center.

▶ **High Backhand Stroke**
A stroke considered difficult but in fact one that can be used to produce clears, drops, and smashes if hit correctly.

FIGURE 7-3 High backhand stroke.

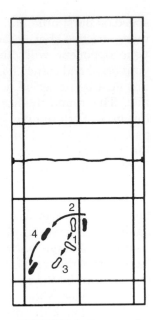

FIGURE 7-4 Footwork to deep backhand corner.

▶ Procedure (See figures 7-4, 7-5, and 7-6)

1. Use the backhand grip, with the ball of the thumb flat against the back bevel of the handle, as described for the backhand drive.
2. Follow the footwork in figure 7-4 to move to the deep left corner. Your right foot should be out front, pointing to the side or back corner, with your back turned partially to the net.
3. At the completion of the backswing, the racket should be well back behind your body with the right elbow pointing up at the shuttle.
4. The most important aspect of the swing for the clear is the timing of the wrist and forearm as they unfold and swing the head of the racket up to meet the shuttle above and just behind the right shoulder. Rather than pulling your whole arm through in a broad stroke, stop your wrist at the highest point, and let the racket whip through in a tight circle centered at your wrist. If you have pulled the racket up to that point with a hard early swing, the racket head will whip through at a great velocity (figure 7-5).
5. If the angle of the racket face is upwards at the point of contact, you will hit a deep clear. If the angle is down, you will hit a smash. To hit a drop, do not let the racket head whip through, but instead guide the shuttle to the net with a slower forearm motion.

FIGURE 7-5 High backhand stroke.

Body not turned far enough sideways   Elbow not pointing up towards shuttle

FIGURE 7-6 Mistakes most commonly made with the high backhand stroke.

6. As you hit the high backhand, your trunk and shoulders will naturally rotate back toward the net as you return to center. Avoid the mistakes shown in figure 7-6.

▶ Strategy

Excellent timing and power are essential on the high backhand to clear the shuttle high enough and deep enough to make it a safe shot. A deep shot to your left side can be played instead with a round-the-head shot, but your court position would be sacrificed. If you can develop an accurate drop and a decent clear off the high backhand, you can prevent an opponent from taking advantage of you on that side. You must assess your capabilities before selecting the shots to use.

THE FLICK SERVE

The **flick serve** is a high serve used almost exclusively in doubles. It is a deceptive alternative to the low serve designed to keep the opponent from rushing your low serve. It will often produce a weak return that can be easily killed. Occasionally it will produce an ace.

▶ Procedure

1. In delivering the serve in doubles, always start with your wrist cocked back at almost a right angle.
2. To deliver a low serve, merely guide the shuttle over the net with a pushing motion of the arm, hardly using the wrist.
3. If you expect the opponent to rush the serve, deliver a flick serve by snapping the wrist through at the last moment, sending the shuttle over the opponent's racket to a point just inside the long doubles service line. (See figure 7-7 for the flight path.)
4. Be careful not to **"balk,"** or use any preliminary faking motions; these are not legal on the serve. Make the two serves look the same until the last moment.

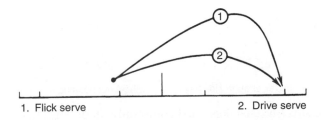

1. Flick serve   2. Drive serve

FIGURE 7-7 Flight patterns of advanced serves in doubles.

Be careful also not to commit a service fault; contact the shuttle *below* your waist and with your hand *above* the racket head.

THE DRIVE SERVE

The **drive serve** is another alternative to the low serve in doubles and can also be useful in singles. Its trajectory is flat, like the drive, and should cramp the receiver by coming into the body quickly (figure 7-7).

▶ Elements of the Drive Serve

1. A weak return is the desired outcome of a good drive serve.
2. Sheer speed and force of shot will not be enough for success.
3. Few points are won outright on the drive serve, or on any serve, because it is played from an underhand (defensive) position.
4. If the drive serve can jolt your opponent off balance and thus place you in an offensive position, the immediate objective has been achieved.
5. The mistake made by an ambitious receiver upon returning a good drive serve is to try to do too much with it. If the shuttle has carried behind the receiver as planned, the receiver should be content to play a safe, high, deep clear to regain balance. This serve will not be so effective if your opponent's reflex speed is exceptionally good.
6. The drive serve may be the answer to serving against a player of different capabilities or against a player whose court position is faulty.

▶ Strategy

The drive serve, most frequently used in doubles, has a specific value to a side-by-side (defensive) team. The angle that can be attained by serving from a position near the sideline can make an aggressive return almost impossible.

▶ **Flick Serve**
A high serve used in doubles to surprise a rushing opponent.

▶ **Balk**
Any deceptive movement that disconcerts an opponent before or during the service; often called a "feint."

▶ **Drive Serve**
A hard, quick serve with a flat trajectory, often used to upset an opponent's pace.

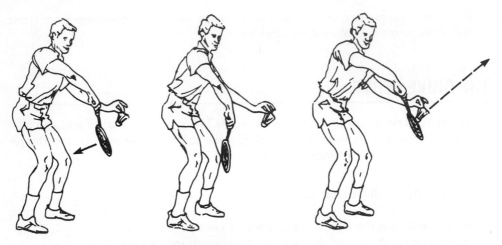

FIGURE 7-8 Backhand serve.

The effectiveness of the drive serve is due to its angle, speed, and some degree of deception. The deception must be in the wrist. Any preliminary movements of the body intended to fool the receiver are illegal on the serve. If the server delays hitting the shuttle for so long as to be unfair to the receiver, it is a fault. This faulty tactic is a balk.

THE BACKHAND SERVE

This serve was developed primarily by Asian players and is now used by many players throughout the world. For a few years, it was used to strike the feathers first with a cutting motion that made the shuttle swerve in flight. The laws now require that the base of the shuttle be hit first on the serve, but the **backhand serve** can still be effective.

▶ Procedure (See figure 7-8)

1. Stand square to the net with your feet side by side, or place the right foot slightly forward.
2. Using a backhand grip, shortened to give more control, hold the racket below your waist and just touching your body.
3. Hold the shuttle by the tips of several feathers in front of your body, with the base pointed toward the racket.
4. Bring the racket forward to stroke the shuttle gently over the net toward the opponent's short service line.
5. If your opponent is rushing the serve too often, you can occasionally use the flick or drive serve on the backhand for a surprise.

▶ **Strategy**

The backhand serve is a useful service variation because:
1. The shuttle is hit in front of the body and takes little time to reach its destination.
2. The shuttle is hard to see against the server's clothes if they are white.

"HOLDING" THE SHUTTLE

▶ **Objective**

The objective of all underhand shots, other than the serve, is to distract the opponent with deceptive moves. A phrase used often by badminton players, **"holding" the shuttle**, refers to pretending to hit the shuttle before you actually do. For example, if you pretend to play a drop, and your opponent moves toward the net, you then flick the shuttle to the backcourt; you have "held" the shot. This type of deception is usually employed with underhand shots. Deception on overhead shots results from preparing to stroke each shot identically as described in chapter 5.

▶ **Procedure**

1. You may "hold" the shot by a feint of the racket, head, or body. It takes time, however, to be deceptive.
2. If you are running at full speed to return the shuttle, there is not time to produce feints! When you find the pace is slower and you have the time, reach forward to play the shuttle; then let it drop and contact it at a lower point.
3. During the time the shuttle is dropping, your opponent may commit to moving forward or back. Be alert to this and either drop or flick the shuttle accordingly.
4. If your opponent is moving too soon and getting caught repeatedly, she or he will be forced to hold position until you contact the shuttle.

▶ **Backhand Serve**
A serve struck with an underhand backhand stroke.

▶ **"Holding" the Shuttle**
Pretending to hit the shuttle but actually delaying the shot to deceive the opponent.

5. Continue to watch the shuttle closely. You will tend to take your eye off the shuttle to see if and in which direction your opponent is moving.

If your errors tell you that you are mishitting and indulging in needless fancy racket work, go back to the basics. If you can master this deception, however, it is a tremendous weapon against a player who is fleet of foot or likes to play a fast game. Slow the game down with defensive shots and then put your deception to work. Try to tire your opponent; then you can apply your pace and power attack.

ADVANCED NET SHOTS AND PLAY

In chapter 5, the hairpin drop was described. There are several other net shots that can be effective when hit from the same position, especially when deceptive techniques such as "holding" the shuttle are employed. These are the net flick, the push shot, and the net smash.

THE NET FLICK

This shot is a valuable alternative to the hairpin drop, especially in singles. It is played at or just below the net level, and the beginning of the stroke should lead the opponent to believe that a hairpin drop is coming. Get to the shuttle early, and reach out to it with the racket head cocked back; in this way, you are "holding" the shuttle. At the last moment, snap your wrist through and send the shuttle to the baseline. See figure 7-9 for the best trajectory.

The **net flick** is particularly effective with an opponent who tends to over-anticipate and rush the net after hitting a drop.

THE PUSH SHOT

The **push shot** is what the name implies—a push, not a stroke. It is played at or above net level with the head of the racket up and the face of the racket flat. Its direction is angled downward. Refer to figure 7-9.

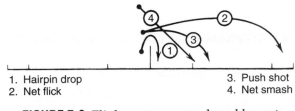

1. Hairpin drop
2. Net flick
3. Push shot
4. Net smash

FIGURE 7-9 Flight patterns produced by net shots.

The use of the push shot, almost nonexistent in singles, becomes highly effective in doubles. When a doubles team takes an up-and-back formation, the shot should be pushed down with a medium amount of speed to the opponent's midcourt. This will place the shuttle just behind the net player and force the backcourt player to reach and stroke the shuttle up. Confusion often results as to which player should return this shot. The push shot cannot be played from below net level.

THE NET SMASH

The other highly important net shot that has to be played above net level is the **net smash.** The shot is accomplished by a downward snap of the wrist. It is the best return of a high, short shot. It is the kill! Care must be taken not to get excessively enthusiastic at the prospect of a setup and bang the shuttle or your racket into the net. Instead, keep your eye on the shuttle and control your swing until the point is completed. The direction of the smash at this close range is not important. If directed straight to the floor with great speed, the smash will be unreturnable (figure 7-9).

STROKES AND STRATEGY

Using the strokes described in chapter 5 and in this chapter in an appropriate sequence, you must outthink your opponent. Preconceived strategy and play are fine until you meet your equal or your supposed superior, in which case your thinking must be spontaneous. Your shots must have speed and control, and the decision as to the pattern or order they take must be made in the fury of the game. In singles, perhaps it will be two clears and then the drop, or clear and drop, and drop again; in doubles, a push shot, a smash, and another smash. In either game catch your opponent going the wrong way by not playing to the obvious open space; because the opponent has moved to that obvious space, play behind him or her. Sometimes you may be caught in your own trap, but if your percentage of

▶ **Net Flick**
An alternative shot to the hairpin drop used especially in singles.

▶ **Push Shot**
A gentle shot played by pushing the shuttle with little wrist motion usually from net or midcourt to the opponent's midcourt.

▶ **Net Smash**
A hard-hitting overhead shot at the net that forces the shuttle sharply downward. It is the best return of a high, short shot.

"catching" is greater than your percentage of being "caught," then you will come out ahead.

If your strokes are well executed and the rallies are long and the play interesting and close, then consider your game successful. That's the fun of the game. Mastery of the strokes will make it possible for you to delight in meeting and pitting your forces against a well-matched opponent. Play with enthusiasm and enjoyment. The winning and the rewards, whatever they may be, will be forthcoming. Reaching this stage of enjoyment comes as a result of concentrated practice.

SUMMARY

- Once the basic strokes are mastered a player can experiment with advanced strokes and shots to heighten the competition.
- The round-the-head stroke is an overhead forehand stroke, but it is played on the backhand side of your body because of the shuttle's position. This may be used instead of a backhand stroke because it is more powerful and deceptive. Yet the ideal player will have just as strong a high backhand stroke, which can be used to produce a clear shot from deep court.
- The flick serve and drive serve are alternatives to the low serve in doubles and can also be used in singles. The backhand serve is also an effective serve.
- The net flick, push shot, and net smash are net shots that can be effective when hit from the same position, especially when the deceptive technique of "holding" the shuttle is employed.

Assessment 7-1

Review of Advanced Strokes

Name _____   Section _____   Date _____

1. Which badminton stroke is considered by many players to be the most difficult? Why is it important to develop your ability to execute this stroke effectively?
2. What mistakes constitute a service fault, and how can each be avoided?
3. In doubles, what is the prime factor determining your choice of shot while you are playing in the "up" position? How does the execution of a smash from this position differ from a smash taken from midcourt?

CHAPTER 8

FACTS
FOR COMPETITORS

▼

OBJECTIVES

After reading this chapter, you will be familiar with competitive opportunities and support services for badminton in the United States and with the organization of badminton in the United States and the world as administered by:

■ USA Badminton.
■ International Badminton Federation.

KEY TERMS

While reading this chapter, you will become familiar with the following terms:

▶ **Badminton USA**
▶ **World Badminton**
▶ Thomas Cup

▶ Uber Cup
▶ World Championships
▶ Sudirman Cup

USA BADMINTON

The governing body for badminton in the United States is USA Badminton (USAB). Through its regional and state associations and member clubs, USAB administers competitive badminton play and promotes the development of badminton in this country. The board of directors of USAB establishes national policies for badminton, and the USAB office is responsible for the day-to-day administration of national badminton activity.

USA Badminton
One Olympic Plaza
Colorado Springs, CO 80909
(719) 578-4808

http://www.usabadminton.org

USAB was founded as the American Badminton Association in 1936, and the current name was adopted in 1998. The general purposes of USAB are these:

1. Promotion and development of badminton play and competition in the United States, without monetary gain.
2. Establishment and upholding of the Laws of Badminton, as adopted by the International Badminton Federation.
3. Arrangement and oversight of the various United States National and Open Championship tournaments.
4. Sanctioning of other tournaments at the local, state, and regional level.
5. Selection and management of players and teams representing the United States in international competitions, including the Olympic Games and the Pan American Games.
6. Representation of the United States and of USAB's interests in activities and decisions of the International Badminton Federation and the United States Olympic Committee.

USAB is worth joining because of these purposes and the many services provided to badminton players at all levels. Some of these services are listed here; further information can be obtained from the national office.

MEMBERSHIP

Membership in USAB is required for participation in USAB sanctioned tournaments and for the right to be considered for national ranking and international competition. There are various categories of membership: Life, Regular, Junior,

► **USA Badminton**

The governing body for badminton in the United States, founded in 1936 as the American Badminton Association and known from 1978 to 1998 as the United States Badminton Association.

Club, and Institution. Life membership is granted to those individuals making a one-time contribution of $500 to USAB, a nonprofit institution incorporated in Colorado; other members pay an annual fee. Life and Regular members may vote and sanction tournaments; all members receive USAB publications.

The Club and Institution categories are group memberships. Each such group receives one vote (in the group name), all USAB publications, and the right to sanction tournaments. Tournament and ranking privileges do not accrue to players in such groups unless they join the USAB individually.

NATIONAL MAGAZINE

The USAB national magazine, *Badminton USA,* is published six times per year. It provides articles of interest to club and tournament players, national rankings, tournament schedules, and results. All USAB members receive *Badminton USA,* but additional subscriptions may be obtained through the national office.

HANDBOOK—RULES BOOK

One of the USAB's most important functions is its responsibility for establishing the rules under which badminton is played in the United States. It therefore publishes the "Official Rules of Play" as part of its official handbook. This is available from the national office at a reasonable price.

VIDEO LIBRARY

USAB maintains an extensive library of badminton videotapes. Many of these show tournament competition between national and world champions; others offer series of badminton instruction. These cassettes may be purchased at reasonable rates.

EQUIPMENT

Although USAB does not sell badminton equipment, other than a small selection of pins, shirts, and sweat clothes, the national office will provide a list of badminton equipment suppliers on request.

CLUBS AND CONTACTS

One publication particularly useful to traveling players is a listing of badminton clubs and contact persons, by zip code, throughout the United States. This list, along with information about badminton play in a particular area, may be obtained from the national office.

EDUCATION FOUNDATION

USAB is aided in its efforts by the United States Badminton Education Foundation (USBEF), established to attract and build endowment support for badminton development programs in this country. Information about the USBEF and how to make gifts to it is available from the USAB office.

BADMINTON CAMPS

Expert instruction over an extended period can be obtained by attending a badminton camp. These camps provide work on strokes, footwork, and conditioning, with the use of video instruction, evaluation, drills, and practice. Also included are informal play with other groups and coaches, suggestions for diet and for care and prevention of athletic injuries, and coaching ideas for large groups. Contact the USAB office for camp information.

PORTABLE BADMINTON COURTS

Several companies, notably Bolltex (Tennis Surfaces Co., Wheaton, IL), Supreme All-Weather Surfaces (Cartersville, GA), and Yonex (Torrance, CA), manufacture portable badminton surfaces. These may be laid out in any gymnasium, hall, or other high-ceilinged room where the floor surface is unsuitable for badminton play. The overall size of each court is about fifty feet-by-twenty-five feet in one or several pieces that may be rolled up and stored. The courts are lined and ready for play and may be obtained with nets and posts and a dolly for handling.

TOURNAMENT SANCTIONS

Tournaments may be sanctioned by obtaining a sanction form from the USAB office, filling it out, and returning it with a sanction fee. The USAB office will provide with the sanction certificate a full packet of information and advice on the running of a successful tournament.

SCHOOL TOURNAMENTS

USAB gives special consideration to schools and colleges regarding sanction fees and membership requirements for tournaments held for students. Contact the USAB office for details.

TOURNAMENTS

Many indoor tournaments are available to those who like real competition. Tournaments are held on various levels: club, school, city, state, regional, intercollegiate, national, and international. Events usually offered are men's singles, women's singles, men's doubles, women's doubles, and mixed doubles. These are held for juniors at various age levels (Under 12, 14, 16, and 19), for adults, and for seniors (veterans) at various age levels (35, 40, 50, 60, and 70 and Over). Many areas classify players into flights designated "A," "B," and "C," so that players compete with others close to their ability; some areas also hold novice tournaments regularly to encourage beginners to compete.

Information regarding dates and locations of tournaments may be found in *Badminton USA* and in badminton newsletters published by local associations. The United States National Championships (adult and senior) are held annually in the spring—March or April, while the National Junior Championships are held in early July. The United States Open Championships, attracting players from around the world, are held each year in the fall—usually September—as part of a North American circuit of tournaments including Canada and Mexico.

The oldest and most famous tournament in the world is the All-England Championship, played in England every March. It was first held in 1899 and attracts hundreds of entrants from around the world. So large and talented is the entry that the qualifying tournament held the week prior is the size of the All-England and is as difficult a tournament as many international open tournaments.

INTERNATIONAL BADMINTON FEDERATION

The International Badminton Federation (IBF) governs international badminton competition throughout the world. The IBF was founded by nine nations in 1934 as an outgrowth of the Badminton Association (of England), which had governed play since 1893. The United States joined in 1938 and has participated actively in all IBF-sponsored competitions since that time. The IBF now has over 140 member nations.

World Badminton is the official on-line publication of the IBF. It contains reports on major tournaments and team competitions held around the world and articles of general interest about badminton. The photographs of top players in action make this electronic publication especially worthwhile (http://www.worldbadminton.net).

International Badminton Federation
Manor Park Place, Rutherford Way
Cheltenham, Gloucestershire
England GL51 9TU
UK
http://www.intbadfed.org

The IBF sponsors four major international competitions:
   Thomas Cup—Men's Team World Championship
   Uber Cup—Ladies' Team World Championship
   World Championships—Individual Competition
   Sudirman Cup—World Team Championships
It is the dream of every young player to represent the United States in one of these events.

THOMAS CUP

The **Thomas Cup** was donated to the IBF in 1939 by Sir George Thomas, one of England's leading badminton and chess players of the early 1900s. His purpose was to create for badminton a men's team competition similar to the Davis Cup in tennis. The competition was delayed by World War II until 1949 and was held triennially for many years, until the decision was made after the 1982 contest to hold the event every two years and to reduce the number of matches in a nation-vs.-nation "tie" from nine to five. Results of the final rounds to date are as follows:

   1948–49 Malaya defeated Denmark, 8–1
   1951–52 Malaya defeated United States, 7–2
   1954–55 Malaya defeated Denmark, 8–1
   1957–58 Indonesia defeated Malaya, 6–3
   1960–61 Indonesia defeated Thailand, 6–3
   1963–64 Indonesia defeated Denmark, 5–4
   1966–67 Malaysia defeated Indonesia, 6–3
   1969–70 Indonesia defeated Malaysia, 6–2
   1972–73 Indonesia defeated Denmark, 8–1
   1975–76 Indonesia defeated Malaysia, 9–0
   1978–79 Indonesia defeated Denmark, 9–0
   1981–82 China defeated Indonesia, 5–4
   1984   Indonesia defeated China, 3–2
   1986   China defeated Indonesia, 3–2
   1988   China defeated Malaysia, 4–1
   1990   China defeated Malaysia, 4–1
   1992   Malaysia defeated Indonesia, 3–2

▶ **World Badminton**
The official on-line publication of the International Badminton Federation (IBF) badminton a competition similar to the Davis Cup in tennis.

▶ **Thomas Cup**
Donated to the IBF in 1939 by Sir George Thomas in hopes it would create for

1994	Indonesia defeated Malaysia, 3–0
1996	Indonesia defeated Denmark, 5–0
1998	Indonesia defeated Malaysia, 3–2
2000	Indonesia defeated China, 3–0

UBER CUP

The Ladies' International Championship for the **Uber Cup** was begun in 1957 with a team trophy donated by one of England's greatest players, Mrs. H. S. (Betty) Uber. Also once held triennially in separate years from the Thomas Cup, the Uber Cup is now contested every two years concurrently with the Thomas Cup. Results of the final rounds to date are as follows:

1956–57	United States defeated Denmark, 6–1
1959–60	United States defeated Denmark, 5–2
1962–63	United States defeated England, 4–3
1965–66	Japan defeated United States, 5–2
1968–69	Japan defeated Indonesia, 6–1
1971–72	Japan defeated Indonesia, 6–1
1974–75	Indonesia defeated Japan, 5–2
1977–78	Japan defeated Indonesia, 5–2
1981–82	Japan defeated Indonesia, 6–3
1984	China defeated England, 5–0
1986	China defeated Indonesia, 5–0
1988	China defeated Korea, 5–0
1990	China defeated Korea, 3–2
1992	China defeated Korea, 3–2
1994	Indonesia defeated China, 3–2
1996	Indonesia defeated China, 4–1
1998	China defeated Indonesia, 4–1
2000	China defeated Denmark, 3–0

The competitions for the Thomas and Uber Cups are held during even-numbered years, and each tie consists of three singles and two doubles matches. Regional playoffs are held in February in several locations around the world, and the winners of these playoffs, along with the defending nations, gather in one location in May or June for the final rounds.

WORLD CHAMPIONSHIPS

The **World Badminton Championships** were initiated in 1977 to provide individual championships complementing the team competitions previously described. They are held in odd-numbered years, alternating with the Cup contests, at sites that vary:

1977—Stockholm
1980—Djakarta
1983—Copenhagen
1985—Calgary
1987—Beijing
1989—Djakarta
1991—Copenhagen
1993—Birmingham, England
1995—Lausanne
1997—Glasgow
1999—Copenhagen

SUDIRMAN CUP

The World Mixed Team Championships were initiated in 1989, to be held in conjunction with the World Championships and to provide competition between teams consisting of men and women. The competition was established in memory of Dick Sudirman, father of Indonesian badminton and IBF vice president. Results to date are as follows:

1989—Indonesia defeated Korea, 3–2
1991—Korea defeated Indonesia, 3–2
1993—Korea defeated Indonesia, 3–2
1995—China defeated Indonesia, 3–1 (last match not played)
1997—China defeated Korea, 5–0
1999—China defeated Denmark, 3–1 (last match not played)

OLYMPIC GAMES

Although badminton was played as a demonstration sport in Munich in 1972 and as an exhibition sport in Seoul in 1988, its Olympic debut as a full medal sport

---

▶ **Uber Cup**

The Ladies' International Championship began in 1957 when one of England's greatest players, Mrs. H. S. Uber, donated a trophy.

▶ **World Championships**

A badminton tournament initiated in 1977 to provide an individual championship complementing the team competitions.

▶ **Sudirman Cup**

A competition established in memory of Dick Sudirman, father of Indonesian badminton and an IBF vice president.

came only in 1992 in Barcelona. The results of the 1992 Olympics and the 1996
Olympics in Atlanta follow.

Barcelona 1992

Men's Singles	Gold:	Alan Budhi Kusuma (Indonesia)
	Silver:	Ardy Wiranata (Indonesia)
	Bronze:	Thomas Stuer-Lauridsen (Denmark)
		Hermawan Susanto (Indonesia)
Women's Singles	Gold:	Susi Susanti (Indonesia)
	Silver:	Bang Soo Hyun (Korea)
	Bronze:	Huang Hua (China)
		Tang Jiuhong (China)
Men's Doubles	Gold:	Park Joo Bong and Moon Soo Kim (Korea)
	Silver:	Eddy Hartono and Rudy Gunawan (Indonesia)
	Bronze:	Li Yongbo and Tian Bingyi (China)
		Razif and Jalani Sidek (Malaysia)
Women's Doubles	Gold:	Hwang Hye Young and Chung So-Young (Korea)
	Silver:	Guan Weizhen and Nong Qunhua (China)
	Bronze:	Lin Yanfen and Yao Fen (China)
		Gil Young-Ah and Shim Eun-Jung (Korea)

Atlanta 1996

Men's Singles	Gold:	Poul-Erik Hoyer-Larsen (Denmark)
	Silver:	Dong Jiong (China)
	Bronze:	Rashid Sidek (Malaysia)
		Heryanto Arbi (Indonesia)
Women's Singles	Gold:	Bang Soo Hyun (Korea)
	Silver:	Mia Audina (Indonesia)
	Bronze:	Kim Ji Hyun (Korea)
		Susi Susanti (Indonesia)
Men's Doubles:	Gold:	Ricky Subagja and Rexy Mainaky (Indonesia)
	Silver:	Cheah Soon Kit and Yap Kim Hok (Malaysia)
	Bronze:	Soo Beng Kiang and Tan Kim Her (Malaysia)
		Denny Kantono and S. Antonius (Indonesia)
Women's Doubles:	Gold:	Ge Fei and Gu Jun (China)
	Silver:	Gil Young Ah and Jang Hye Ock (Korea)
	Bronze:	Qin Yiyuan and Tang Yongshu (China)
		Helene Kierkegaard and Rikke Olsen (Denmark)
Mixed Doubles:	Gold:	Kim Dong Moon and Gil Young Ah (Korea)
	Silver:	Park Joo Bong and Ra Kyung Min (Korea)
	Bronze:	Liu Jianjun and Sun Man (China)
		Chen Xingdong and Peng Xingyong (China)

SUMMARY

- There are numerous (national and international) competitive opportunities for badminton players.
- USA Badminton is the governing body for badminton in the United States, whose purpose is to promote and develop badminton, uphold the Laws of Badminton, oversee tournaments, and represent the United States in international activities.
- The International Badminton Federation (IBF) governs the international badminton competition throughout the world. It sponsors four major international competitions: Thomas Cup (Men's Team), Uber Cup (Women's Team), World Championship (Individual), and Sudirman Cup (World Team).

CHAPTER 9

DRILLS AND CONDITIONING

OBJECTIVES

After reading this chapter, you will know the shot patterns of twelve drills designed to add accuracy and consistency to:

- Clears.
- Drops.
- Smashes.
- Drives.

Two additional drills are specifically geared to developing greater endurance.

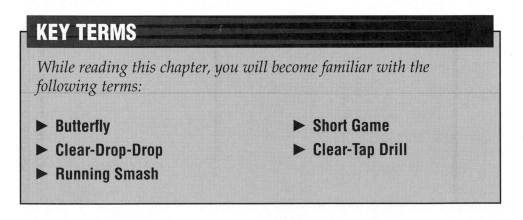

KEY TERMS

While reading this chapter, you will become familiar with the following terms:

▶ **Butterfly**

▶ **Clear-Drop-Drop**

▶ **Running Smash**

▶ **Short Game**

▶ **Clear-Tap Drill**

The first step in learning badminton, understanding the why and how of stroke development, must be followed by stroke practice. No amount of intellectual grasp of the game can substitute for either repetitive practice of the stroke pattern or coordination of the racket and shuttle to assure correct timing. Mental and physical processes should work together to speed up progress.

Badminton is a game requiring great stamina. The shot drills described here are a good start for building the fitness required for badminton, but it is advisable to do more. This chapter also contains suggestions for a conditioning program suited to badminton.

SHOT DRILLS

Various drills and suggestions for individual improvement are given in this chapter. In the diagrams that follow, a solid line (_____) indicates the path of the shuttle, while a broken line (-------) indicates the movement of the players. To make your drills most successful, locate another player with approximately the same degree of skill; neither player benefits sufficiently if the range of skill varies too greatly.

BUTTERFLY DRILL

This drill gets its name from the flight pattern of the shuttle (figure 9-1). It is a good drill to begin with because it does not call for "all-out" hitting or running. Player A serves low to the outside corner of B's service court; B replies with a halfcourt down-the-line. A hits a crosscourt halfcourt, and B again replies with a straight halfcourt. This pattern of halfcourts continues: straight, crosscourt, straight, crosscourt, and so on. Players can then reverse roles for balanced practice.

OVERHEAD CLEAR DRILL

Both players take their center positions where the drill for the clear starts with a singles serve and thereafter continues with clears only (figure 9-2). The clears should first be played parallel to the sideline, then crosscourt, then alternating

▶ **Butterfly**
   A drill flight pattern: straight, crosscourt,
   straight, crosscourt, and so on.

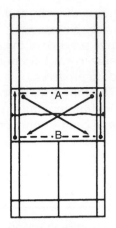

FIGURE 9-1
Butterfly drill.

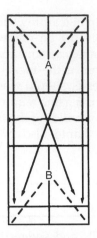

FIGURE 9-2
Overhead
clear drill.

straight and crosscourt, giving each player a chance to clear from both deep corners. The shuttle should be directed repeatedly to the same corner before changing the direction to the other corner. The player stroking from the backhand should use an overhead backhand or round-the-head clear. The object is to repeatedly clear the shuttle high and deep from one corner to an opposite corner between the doubles and singles back boundary line. Returning to center position after each hit develops good footwork and stamina.

HINT: Get behind and in line with the shuttle for increased depth. Upon contact, step and move your weight toward the net.

SERVE DRILL

Perfecting the serve, one of the easiest strokes to practice, can be done with or without a partner. Collect about twenty shuttles, which will permit you to take your service position for twenty strokes before retrieving shuttles. This not only saves time but also adds to the consistency of your stroke. The serve, whether for singles or doubles, should be directed to a particular corner on the court. Practice to all corners for singles and doubles. Even if a partner is present, the serve should not be returned; instead, it should be allowed to fall to the court, enabling the server to see exactly how close to the target the shuttle came.

HINT: Drop the shuttle well away from you to get freedom of movement, which will result in better accuracy.

OVERHEAD DROP AND UNDERHAND CLEAR DRILL

Both players begin in the center position from which the drill starts with a singles serve by A to a back corner (figure 9-3). The receiver, B, returns it with an overhead drop to a front corner. An underhand clear to the same back corner follows and the drill continues: drop, clear, drop, clear, until one player fails to return the shuttle. The shuttle should be directed repeatedly to the same corner until there is some degree of control before switching the direction of the shuttle to another front or back corner. Again, both players should return to the center position if the drill is to simulate game conditions.

HINT: B should pretend to stroke an overhead clear, and A a hairpin drop, to acquire the deception needed for the two shots hit.

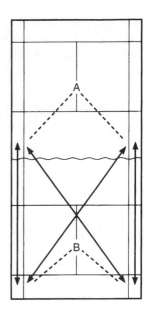

FIGURE 9-3 Overhead drop and underhand clear drill.

SMASH AND UNDERHAND CLEAR DRILL

This drill, much like the preceding drop and clear drill, begins with a singles serve by A to either back corner (figure 9-4). The smash by B, either parallel to the sideline or crosscourt to the opposite midcourt, is returned with a high underhand clear. The drill then becomes smash, clear, smash, clear, until either player misses; the drill then begins again from center with the serve.

HINT: To eliminate faulty shots, start with slower smashes and gradually increase the speed of your smash.

CLEAR-DROP-DROP DRILL

The shots in this drill are hit down-the-line, so two pairs of players can share a court for the drill (figure 9-5). The three-shot pattern means that roles reverse with each cycle in the drill. Player A hits an underhand clear high to B, B hits an

▶ **Clear-Drop-Drop**
Shots in this drill are hit down-the-line.

overhead drop, and A responds with a net drop. Here the roles reverse: B runs in to hit a clear (underhand), A hits an overhead drop, and B hits a net drop. The drill continues as it started with A hitting an underhand clear.

CLEAR-SMASH-DROP DRILL

This drill is similar to the clear-drop-drop drill. Instead of hitting an overhead drop off the clear, B hits a straight smash instead, and A responds with an underhand drop. The pattern continues with B clearing so that A can smash.

RUNNING SMASH

This drill is a simple variation of the clear-smash-drop drill, and it requires the entire court (figure 9-6). The shot pattern is still clear-smash-drop, but while the smash and drop are hit straight, the clear is hit crosscourt. This drill is particularly good practice for the round-the-head smash.

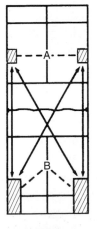

FIGURE 9-4 Smash and underhand clear drill.

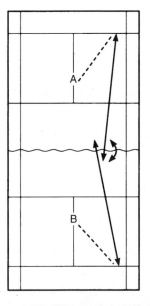

FIGURE 9-5 Clear-drop-drop drill.

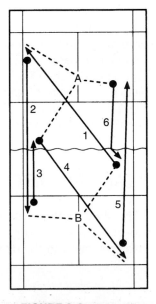

FIGURE 9-6 Running smash drill.

FOUR CLEAR-TWO DROP DRILL

This drill also requires the entire court and has a six-shot pattern: four straight clears, one overhead crosscourt drop, one straight net drop (figure 9-7). Player A clears to B in one deep corner, B clears, A clears, and B clears, all straight. Then, A hits a crosscourt drop, which B runs in to return with a net drop straight. Player A runs in to clear out to B's deep corner, starting the next cycle. Players can reverse roles for balanced practice.

DRIVE DRILL

There are four drives to be practiced: the straight (parallel to the sideline) forehand and backhand, and the crosscourt forehand and backhand (figure 9-8). This drill begins with both players in the center of the court. Player A hits a drive serve to the predetermined forehand or backhand of B. Continue with repeated drives of the same shot. Each of the four drives—forehand to forehand; backhand to backhand; forehand to backhand; and backhand to forehand—should be practiced repeatedly before the side and direction are changed. Little backswing should be used for these drives; punch the shuttle with a quick wrist motion. Return to center after each hit.

HINT: Contact the drive high so that this drill does not become a smash and clear drill.

SHORT GAME

This game, played and scored exactly according to singles rules, begins with a low serve by A and return of serve at the net by B: thereafter, only net shots, straight or crosscourt, can be played (figure 9-9). Any shots, other than the serve, that fall behind the short service line are considered out of court. This drill, valuable to beginners learning rules and scoring, develops the forecourt skill and judgment necessary in doubles and mixed doubles.

HINT: Stand far enough away from the net to give yourself time and space to stroke properly.

► **Running Smash**
A simple variation of the clear-smash-drop drill.

► **Short Game**
A good drill that resembles singles play because it involves following badminton's rules and scoring.

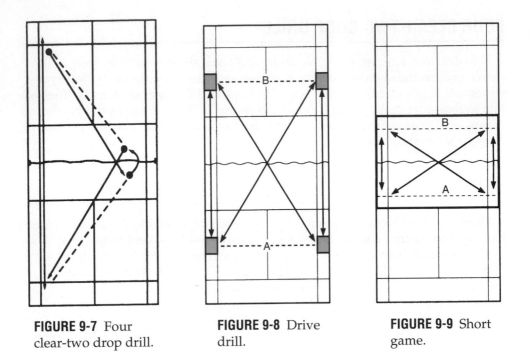

FIGURE 9-7 Four
clear-two drop drill.

FIGURE 9-8 Drive
drill.

FIGURE 9-9 Short
game.

THREE STROKE DRILL

The first three shots of a rally, important because the offense or defense may easily be determined with initial shots, should be practiced and a decision made after each sequence as to the effectiveness of the serve, return of serve, and the third shot.

HINT: Try to be in an offensive position after the third shot.

ENDURANCE CONDITIONING

Whether you are able to finish your match or practice period in good fashion, that is, still stroking the shuttle with power and control, is determined largely by your physical condition. The player in poor condition begins to make errors and slow down after a short time. Badminton should be a game of long, interesting rallies free from outright errors, and this demands strength and endurance.

There are various ways of improving your endurance. Distance running, soccer, hockey, basketball—all the running games—are of value. Modern dance, gymnastics, and rope skipping add quickness and flexibility. Tennis, racketball, and squash, closely related to badminton, require some strokes similar to the badminton player's game. Care must be given, however, not to adopt the firm wrist and longer backswings of these other racket sports. Table tennis is excellent for improving reflexes. All these activities contribute to the conditioning process, but the best conditioning for badminton is to play badminton. If you rehearse your stroke practice drills properly by returning to center position between each stroke, you will develop endurance. Practice games against someone of exact equal ability will result in long, endurance-demanding rallies.

Tobacco and alcohol negatively affect your physical condition. Adequate sleep and food supply the energy reserve needed to meet the demands of a strenuous game.

Here are several on-court drills effective in building fitness for badminton.

CLEAR-TAP DRILL

This drill is effective in developing stamina for long rallies, and two pairs can share the court. The drill consists entirely of overhead clears, but between hitting clears, each player must run in to tap his or her racket on the short service line. You quickly find that it pays to be moving forward as you clear and to hit your clears sufficiently high and deep.

UNEQUAL PARTNER DRILL

Many times good players unable to find opponents of like skill can devise ways of using beginners as practice partners (figure 9-10). For instance, the advanced player (A) strokes the shuttle to one corner of the court to the beginner (B) who may then return the shuttle any place on the court. The advanced player develops control by playing the shuttle to the beginner's racket, thus enabling the rally to continue. The advanced player develops footwork, stamina, and stroke control chasing the comparatively uncontrolled returns of the novice. This drill can be amusing and fun to two players who desire to learn (each at his or her own level) and are willing to cooperate.

HINT: Enjoy the practice as if it were a game.

FIGURE 9-10
Unequal
partner drill.

▶ **Clear-Tap Drill**

A drill that consists entirely of overhead clears, but between hitting clears each player must run to tap the racket on the short service line.

SUMMARY

- The shot drills should be practiced to improve not only fitness but also stroke development. Pick another badminton player with your same skill level; neither player sufficiently benefits if the range of skills varies too greatly. Use the following drills to practice: butterfly, overhead clear, serve, overhead drop and underhand clear, smash and underhand clear, clear-drop-drop, clear-smash-drop, running smash, four clear-two drop, drive, short game, and three stroke.
- For more fitness oriented fills practice the clear-tap drill or unequal partner drill.

Appendix A

DEFINITIONS

Player	Any person playing badminton
Match	The basic contest in badminton between opposing sides each of 1 or 2 players
Singles	A match where there is one player on each of the opposing sides
Doubles	A match where there are two players on each of the opposing sides
Serving side	The side having the right to serve
Receiving side	The side opposing the serving side

1. COURT AND COURT EQUIPMENT

1.1 The court shall be a rectangle laid out with lines 40 mm wide as in Diagram A.
1.2 The lines shall be easily distinguishable and preferably be coloured white or yellow.
1.3 All lines form part of the area which they define.
1.4 The posts shall be 1.55 metres in height from the surface of the court and shall remain vertical when the net is strained as provided in Law 1.10.
1.5 The posts shall be placed on the doubles side lines as in Diagram A irrespective of whether singles or doubles is being played.
1.6 The net shall be made of fine cord of dark colour and even thickness with a mesh of not less than 15 mm and not more than 20 mm.
1.7 The net shall be 760 mm in depth and at least 6.1 metres wide.
1.8 The top of the net shall be edged with a 75 mm white cloth tape doubled over a cord or cable running through the tape. This tape must rest upon the cord or cable.
1.9 The cord or cable shall be stretched firmly, flush with the top of the posts.
1.10 The top of the net from the surface of the court shall be 1.524 metres at the centre of the court and 1.55 metres over the side lines for doubles.

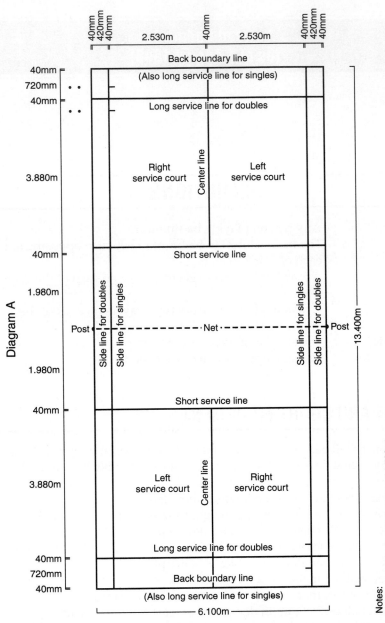

Diagram A

40mm
420mm
40mm
2.530m
40mm
2.530m
40mm
420mm
40mm

Back boundary line

40mm
(Also long service line for singles)

720mm

40mm
Long service line for doubles

Right service court

Center line

Left service court

3.880m

40mm
Short service line

1.980m

Side line for doubles

Side line for singles

Post — — — — — — Net — — — — — — Post

Side line for singles

Side line for doubles

13.400m

1.980m

40mm
Short service line

Left service court

Center line

Right service court

3.880m

Long service line for doubles

40mm

720mm

40mm
Back boundary line

(Also long service line for singles)

6.100m

Notes:
1. Diagonal length of full court = 14.723m
2. Court as shown can be used for both singles and doubles play
3. Optional testing marks shown in Diagram B

1.11 There shall be no gaps between the ends of the net and the posts. If necessary, the full depth of the net should be tied at the ends.

2. SHUTTLE

2.1 The shuttle may be made from natural and/or synthetic materials. From whatever material the shuttle is made, the flight characteristics generally should be similar to those produced by a natural feathered shuttle with a cork base covered by a thin layer of leather.

2.2 The shuttle shall have 16 feathers fixed in the base.

2.3 The feathers shall be measured from the tip to the top of the base and in each shuttle shall be of the same length. This length can be between 62 mm and 70 mm.

2.4 The tips of the feathers shall lie on a circle with a diameter from 58 mm to 68 mm.

2.5 The feathers shall be fastened firmly with thread or other suitable material.

2.6 The base shall be 25 mm to 28 mm in diameter and rounded on the bottom.

2.7 The shuttle shall weigh from 4.74 to 5.50 grams.

2.8 *Non-Feathered Shuttle*

    2.8.1 The skirt, or simulation of feathers in synthetic materials, replaces natural feathers.

    2.8.2 The base is described in Law 2.6.

    2.8.3 Measurements and weight shall be as in Laws 2.3, 2.4 and 2.7. However, because of the difference in the specific gravity and other properties of synthetic materials in comparison with feathers, a variation of up to 10 per cent is acceptable.

2.9 Subject to there being no variation in the general design, speed and flight of the shuttle, modifications in the above specifications may be made with the approval of the Member Association concerned:

    2.9.1 in places where atmospheric conditions due to either altitude or climate make the standard shuttle unsuitable; or

    2.9.2 if special circumstances exist which make it otherwise necessary in the interests of the game.

3. TESTING A SHUTTLE FOR SPEED

3.1 To test a shuttle, use a full underhand stroke which makes contact with the shuttle over the back boundary line. The shuttle shall be hit at an upward angle and in a direction parallel to the side lines.

3.2 A shuttle of correct speed will land not less than 530 mm and not more than 990 mm short of the other back boundary line as in Diagram B.

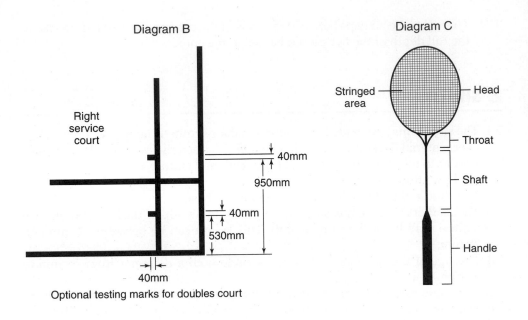

Diagram B

Right
service
court

40mm
950mm
40mm
530mm

40mm

Optional testing marks for doubles court

Diagram C

Stringed
area

Head

Throat

Shaft

Handle

4. RACKET

4.1 The parts of a racket are described in Laws 4.1.1 to 4.1.7 and are illustrated in Diagram C.

    4.1.1 The main racket parts are called the handle, the stringed area, the head, the shaft, the throat and the frame.

    4.1.2 The handle is the part of the racket intended to be gripped by the player.

    4.1.3 The stringed area is the part of the racket with which it is intended the player hits the shuttle.

    4.1.4 The head bounds the stringed area.

    4.1.5 The shaft connects the handle to the head (subject to Law 4.1.6).

    4.1.6 The throat (if present) connects the shaft to the head.

    4.1.7 The frame is the name given to the head, throat, shaft and handle taken together.

4.2 The frame of the racket shall not exceed 680 mm in overall length and 230 mm in overall width.

4.3 *Stringed area*

    4.3.1 The stringed area shall be flat and consist of a pattern of crossed strings either alternately interlaced or bonded where they cross. The stringing pattern shall be generally uniform and, in particular, not less dense in the centre than in any other area.

    4.3.2 The stringed area shall not exceed 280 mm in overall length and 220 mm in overall width. However, the strings may extend into an area which otherwise would be the throat, provided that the width of the extended stringed area does not exceed 35 mm and provided that the overall length of the stringed area does not then exceed 330 mm.

4.4 *The racket:*

4.4.1 shall be free of attached objects and protrusions, other than those used solely and specifically to limit or prevent wear and tear, or vibration, or to distribute weight, or to secure the handle by cord to the player's hand, and which are reasonable in size and placement for such purposes; and

4.4.2 shall be free of any device which makes it possible for a player to change materially the shape of the racket.

5. EQUIPMENT COMPLIANCE

The International Badminton Federation shall rule on any question of whether any racket, shuttle or equipment or any prototype used in the playing of badminton complies with the specifications. Such ruling may be undertaken on the Federation's initiative or upon application by any party with a bona fide interest therein, including any player, equipment manufacturer or Member Association or member thereof.

6. TOSS

6.1 Before play commences, a toss shall be conducted and the side winning the toss shall exercise the choice in either Law 6.1.1 or 6.1.2:

6.1.1 to serve or receive first;

6.1.2 to start play at one end of the court or the other.

6.2 The side losing the toss shall then exercise the remaining choice.

7. SCORING SYSTEM

7.1 A match shall consist of the best of three games, unless otherwise arranged.

7.2 In doubles and men's singles a game is won by the first side to score 15 points, except as provided in Law 7.4.

7.3 In ladies' singles a game is won by the first side to score 11 points, except as provided in Law 7.4.

7.4 If the score becomes 14-all (10-all in ladies' singles), the side which first scored 14(10) shall exercise the choice in Law 7.4.1 or 7.4.2:

7.4.1 to continue the game to 15(11) points, i.e., not to 'set' the game; or

7.4.2 to 'set' the game to 17(13) points.

7.5 The side winning a game serves first in the next game.

7.6 Only the serving side can add a point to its score (see Law 10.3 or 11.4).

8. CHANGE OF ENDS

8.1 Players shall change ends:
    8.1.1 at the end of the first game;
    8.1.2 prior to the beginning of the third game (if any); and
    8.1.3 in the third game, or in a match of one game, when the leading score reaches:
        —6 in a game of 11 points; or
        —8 in a game of 15 points.
8.2 If players omit to change ends as indicated in Law 8.1, they shall do so as soon as the mistake is discovered and the shuttle is not in play. The existing score shall stand.

9. SERVICE

9.1 In a correct service:
    9.1.1 neither side shall cause undue delay to the delivery of the service once server and receiver have taken up their respective positions;
    9.1.2 the server and receiver shall stand within diagonally opposite service courts without touching the boundary lines of these service courts;
    9.1.3 some part of both feet of the server and receiver must remain in contact with the surface of the court in a stationary position from the start of the service (Law 9.4) until the service is delivered (Law 9.6);
    9.1.4 the server's racket shall initially hit the base of the shuttle;
    9.1.5 the whole shuttle shall be below the server's waist at the instant of being hit by the server's racket;
    9.1.6 the shaft of the server's racket at the instant of hitting the shuttle shall be pointing in a downward direction to such an extent that the whole of the head of the racket is discernibly below the whole of the server's hand holding the racket as in Diagram D;
    9.1.7 the movement of the server's racket must continue forwards after the start of the service (Law 9.4) until the service is delivered; and
    9.1.8 the flight of the shuttle shall be upwards from the server's racket to pass over the net so that, if not intercepted, it lands in the receiver's service court (i.e., on or within the boundary lines).
9.2 If a service is not correct by virtue of any of Laws 9.1.1 to 9.1.8, it shall be a 'fault' (Law 13) by the offending side.
9.3 It is a 'fault' if the server, in attempting to serve, misses the shuttle.
9.4 Once the players have taken their positions, the first forward movement of the server's racket head is the start of the service.
9.5 The server shall not serve before the receiver is ready but the receiver shall be considered to have been ready if a return of service is attempted.
9.6 Once the service is started (Law 9.4), it is delivered when the shuttle is hit by the server's racket or, in attempting to serve, the server misses the shuttle.

Diagram D

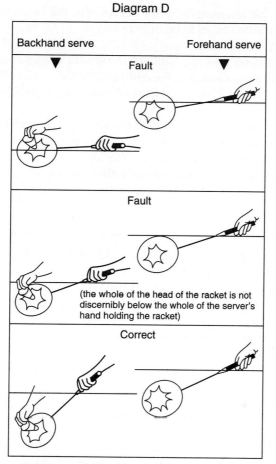

Backhand serve   Forehand serve

Fault

Fault

(the whole of the head of the racket is not discernibly below the whole of the server's hand holding the racket)

Correct

Positions of the racket and of the server's hand
holding it at the instant of striking the shuttle

9.7 In doubles, the partners may take up any positions which do not unsight the opposing server or receiver.

10. SINGLES

10.1 *Serving and receiving courts*

     10.1.1 The players shall serve from, and receive in, their respective right service courts when the server has not scored or has scored an even number of points in that game.

     10.1.2 The players shall serve from, and receive in, their respective left service courts when the server has scored an odd number of points in that game.

10.2 The shuttle is hit alternately by the server and the receiver until a 'fault' is made or the shuttle ceases to be in play.

10.3 *Scoring and serving*

    10.3.1 If the receiver makes a 'fault' or the shuttle ceases to be in play because it touches the surface of the court inside the receiver's court, the server scores a point. The server then serves again from the alternate service court.

    10.3.2 If the server makes a 'fault' or the shuttle ceases to be in play because it touches the surface of the court inside the server's court, the server loses the right to continue serving and the receiver then becomes the server, with no point scored by either player.

11. DOUBLES

11.1 At the start of a game, and each time a side gains the right to serve, the service shall be delivered from the right service court.

11.2 Only the receiver shall return the service: should the shuttle touch or be hit by the receiver's partner, it shall be a 'fault' and the serving side scores a point.

11.3 *Order of play and position on court*

    11.3.1 After the service is returned, the shuttle may be hit by either player of the serving side and then by either player of the receiving side, and so on, until the shuttle ceases to be in play.

    11.3.2 After the service is returned, a player may hit the shuttle from any position on that player's side of the net.

11.4 *Scoring and serving*

    11.4.1 If the receiving side makes a 'fault' or the shuttle ceases to be in play because it touches the surface of the court inside the receiving side's court, the serving side scores a point and the server serves again.

    11.4.2 If the serving side makes a 'fault' or the shuttle ceases to be in play because it touches the surface of the court inside the serving side's court, the server loses the right to continue serving, with no point scored by either side.

11.5 *Serving and receiving courts*

    11.5.1 The player who serves at the start of any game shall serve from, or receive in, the right service court when that player's side has not scored or has scored an even number of points in that game, and the left service court when that player's side has scored an odd number of points in that game.

    11.5.2 The player who receives at the start of any game shall receive in, or serve from, the right service court when that player's side has not scored or has scored an even number of points in that game, and the left service court when that player's side has scored an odd number of points in that game.

    11.5.3 The reverse pattern shall apply to the partners.

11.6 Service in any turn of serving shall be delivered from alternate service courts, except as provided in Laws 12 and 14.

11.7 In any game, the right to serve passes consecutively from the initial server to the initial receiver, then to that initial receiver's partner, then to the opponent who is due to serve from the right service court (Law 11.5), then to that player's partner, and so on.

11.8 No player shall serve out of turn, receive out of turn, or receive two consecutive services in the same game, except as provided in Laws 12 and 14.

11.9 Either player of the winning side may serve first in the next game, and either player of the losing side may receive.

12. SERVICE COURT ERRORS

12.1 A service court error has been made when a player:
   12.1.1 has served out of turn;
   12.1.2 has served from the wrong service court; or
   12.1.3 standing in the wrong service court, was prepared to receive the service and it has been delivered.

12.2 If a service court error is discovered after the next service has been delivered, the error shall not be corrected.

12.3 If a service court error is discovered before the next service is delivered:
   12.3.1 if both sides committed an error, it shall be a 'let';
   12.3.2 if one side committed the error and won the rally, it shall be a 'let';
   12.3.3 if one side committed the error and lost the rally, the error shall not be corrected.

12.4 If there is a 'let' because of a service court error, the rally is replayed with the error corrected.

12.5 If a service court error is not to be corrected, play in that game shall proceed without changing the players' new service courts (nor, when relevant, the new order of serving).

13. FAULTS

It is a 'fault':

13.1 if a service is not correct (Law 9.1) or if Law 9.3 or 11.2 applies;

13.2 if in play, the shuttle:
   13.2.1 lands outside the boundaries of the court (i.e., not on or within the boundary lines);
   13.2.2 passes through or under the net;
   13.2.3 fails to pass the net;
   13.2.4 touches the ceiling or side walls;
   13.2.5 touches the person or dress of a player; or

13.2.6 touches any other object or person outside the immediate surroundings of the court;

(Where necessary on account of the structure of the building, the local badminton authority may, subject to the right of veto of its Member Association, make bye-laws dealing with cases in which a shuttle touches an obstruction).

13.3 if, when in play, the initial point of contact with the shuttle is not on the striker's side of the net. (The striker may, however, follow the shuttle over the net with the racket in the course of a stroke);

13.4 if, when the shuttle is in play, a player:

13.4.1 touches the net or its supports with racket, person or dress;

13.4.2 invades an opponent's court over the net with racket or person except as permitted in Law 13.3;

13.4.3 invades an opponent's court under the net with racket or person such that an opponent is obstructed or distracted; or

13.4.4 obstructs an opponent, i.e., prevents an opponent from making a legal stroke where the shuttle is followed over the net;

13.5 if, in play, a player deliberately distracts an opponent by any action such as shouting or making gestures;

13.6 if, in play, the shuttle:

13.6.1 is caught and held on the racket and then slung during the execution of a stroke;

13.6.2 is hit twice in succession by the same player with two strokes;

13.6.3 is hit by a player and the player's partner successively; or

13.6.4 touches a player's racket and continues towards the back of that player's court;

13.7 if a player is guilty of flagrant, repeated or persistent offences under Law 16;

13.8 if, on service, the shuttle is caught on the net and remains suspended on top or, on service, after passing over the net is caught in the net.

14. LETS

14.1 'Let' is called by the umpire, or by a player (if there is no umpire), to halt play.

14.2 A 'let' may be given for any unforeseen or accidental occurrence.

14.3 If a shuttle is caught on the net and remains suspended on top or, after passing over the net, is caught in the net, it shall be a 'let' except on service.

14.4 If, during service, the receiver and server are both faulted at the same time, it shall be a 'let'.

14.5 If the server serves before the receiver is ready, it shall be a 'let'.

14.6 If, during play, the shuttle disintegrates and the base completely separates from the rest of the shuttle, it shall be a 'let'.

14.7 If a line judge is unsighted and the umpire is unable to make a decision, it shall be a 'let'.

14.8 A 'let' may occur following a service court error; see Law 12.3.

14.9 When a 'let' occurs, the play since the last service shall not count and the player who served shall serve again, except where Law 12 is applicable.

15. SHUTTLE NOT IN PLAY

A shuttle is not in play when:

15.1 it strikes the net and remains attached there or suspended on top;

15.2 it strikes the net or post and starts to fall towards the surface of the court on the striker's side of the net;

15.3 it hits the surface of the court; or

15.4 a 'fault' or 'let' has occurred.

16. CONTINUOUS PLAY, MISCONDUCT, PENALTIES

16.1 Play shall be continuous from the first service until the match is concluded, except as allowed in Laws 16.2 and 16.3.

16.2 Intervals not exceeding 90 seconds between the first and second games, and not exceeding 5 minutes between the second and third games, are allowed in all matches in all of the following situations:

    16.2.1 international competitive events;

    16.2.2 IBF-sanctioned events; and

    16.2.3 all other matches unless the Member Association has previously published a decision not to allow such intervals.

(In televised matches the Referee may decide before the match that intervals as in Law 16.2 are mandatory and of fixed duration).

16.3 *Suspension of play*

    16.3.1 When necessitated by circumstances not within the control of the players, the umpire may suspend play for such a period as the umpire may consider necessary.

    16.3.2 Under special circumstances the Referee may instruct the umpire to suspend play.

    16.3.3 If play is suspended, the existing score shall stand and play shall be resumed from that point.

16.4 Under no circumstances shall play be delayed to enable a player to recover strength or wind.

16.5 *Advice and leaving the court*

    16.5.1 Except in the intervals provided in Laws 16.2 and 16.3, no player shall be permitted to receive advice during a match.

    16.5.2 Except during the five minute interval described in Law 16.2, no player shall leave the court during a match without the umpire's permission.

16.6 The umpire shall be the sole judge of any delay in play.

16.7 A player shall not:

    16.7.1 deliberately cause delay in, or suspension of, play;

    16.7.2 deliberately modify or damage the shuttle in order to change its speed or its flight;

    16.7.3 behave in an offensive manner; or

    16.7.4 be guilty of misconduct not otherwise covered by the Laws of badminton.

16.8 The umpire shall administer any breach of Law 16.4, 16.5 or 16.7 by:

    16.8.1 issuing a warning to the offending side;

    16.8.2 faulting the offending side, if previously warned; or

    16.8.3 in cases of flagrant offence or persistent offences, faulting the offending side and reporting the offending side immediately to the Referee, who shall have power to disqualify the offending side from the match.

17. OFFICIALS AND APPEALS

17.1 The Referee is in overall charge of the tournament or event of which a match forms part.

17.2 The umpire, where appointed, is in charge of the match, the court and its immediate surrounds. The umpire shall report to the Referee.

17.3 The service judge shall call service faults made by the server should they occur (Law 9).

17.4 A line judge shall indicate whether a shuttle landed 'in' or 'out' on the line(s) assigned.

17.5 An official's decision is final on all points of fact for which that official is responsible.

17.6 An umpire shall:

    17.6.1 uphold and enforce the Laws of badminton and, especially, call a 'fault' or 'let' should either occur;

    17.6.2 give a decision on any appeal regarding a point of dispute, if made before the next service is delivered;

    17.6.3 ensure players and spectators are kept informed of the progress of the match;

    17.6.4 appoint or remove line judges or a service judge in consultation with the Referee;

    17.6.5 where another court official is not appointed, arrange for that official's duties to be carried out;

    17.6.6 where an appointed official is unsighted, carry out the official's duties or play a 'let';

    17.6.7 record and report to the Referee all matters in relation to Law 16; and

    17.6.8 take to the Referee all unsatisfied appeals on questions of law only. (Such appeals must be made before the next service is delivered or, if at the end of the game, before the side that appeals has left the court).

VARIATIONS IN COURT AND EQUIPMENT

1. Where it is not practicable to have posts on the sidelines, some method must be used to indicate the position of the sidelines where they pass under the net, e.g., by the use of thin posts or strips of material 40 mm wide, fixed to the side lines and rising vertically to the net cord.

2. Where space does not permit the marking out of a court for doubles, a court may be marked out for singles only as shown in Diagram E. The back boundary

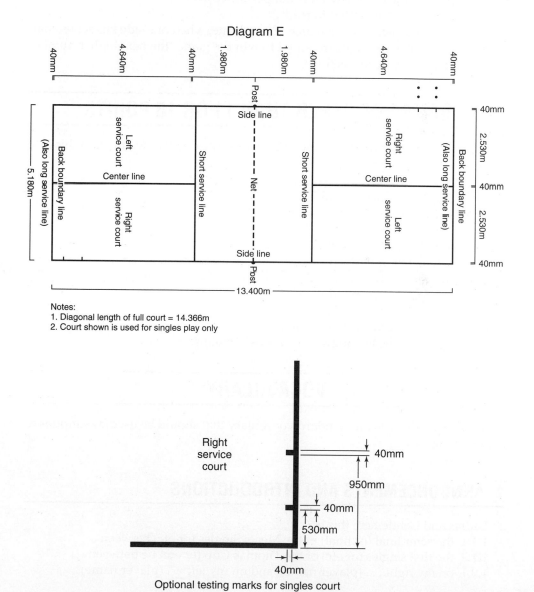

Diagram E

Notes:
1. Diagonal length of full court = 14.366m
2. Court shown is used for singles play only

Optional testing marks for singles court

lines become also the long service lines and the posts or the strips of material representing them shall be placed on the side lines.

HANDICAP MATCHES

In handicap matches, the following variations in the Laws apply:

1.1 No variation is permitted in the number of points required to win a game (i.e., setting the game as in Law 7.4 is not permitted).

1.2 Law 8.1.3 will be amended to read:
'in the third game, and in a match of one game, when one side has scored half the total number of points required to win the game (the next higher number being taken in case of fractions).'

GAMES OF OTHER THAN 11 OR 15 POINTS

It is permissible to play one game of 21 points by prior arrangement. In this case the following variations apply:

1. Law 7.2 shall be amended, replacing 15 with 21.
2. Law 7.3 shall be amended, replacing 11 with 21.
3. Law 7.4 shall be amended to read:
    '7.4 If the score becomes 20-all, the side which first scored 20 shall exercise the choice in Law 7.4.1 or 7.4.2:'
4. Law 7.4.1 shall be amended to read:
    '7.4.1 to continue the game to 21 points, i.e., not to 'set' the game; or'
5. Law 7.4.2 shall be amended to read:
    '7.4.2 to 'set' the game to 23 points.'
6. Law 8.1.3 shall be amended to read:
    '8.1.3 . . . when the leading score reaches 11 points.'

VOCABULARY

(This Appendix lists the standard vocabulary that should be used by umpires to control a match.)

1. ANNOUNCEMENTS AND INTRODUCTIONS

1. Ladies and Gentlemen, this is:
    1.1.1 the semi-final (or final) of the Men's Singles (or etc) between
    1.1.2 the first singles (or etc) of the Thomas Cup (or etc) tie between
    1.2.1 on my right . . . (player name), and on my left . . . (player name)

1.2.2 on my right . . . (country/team name), represented by . . . (player name), and on my left . . . (country/team name), represented by . . . (player name)

1.3.1 . . . (player name) to serve

1.3.2 . . . (country/team name) to serve

1.4.1 . . . (player name) to serve to . . . (player name)

1.4.2 . . . (player name) to . . . (player name)'

2. START OF MATCH AND CALLING THE SCORE

2.1 'Love all; play'

2.2 'Service over'

2.3 'Second server'

2.4 '. . . game point . . .' e.g., '14 game point 6', or '16 game point 14'

2.5 '. . . match point . . .' e.g., '14 match point 8', or '16 match point 14'

2.6 '. . . game point all . . .' e.g., '14 game point all', or '16 game point all'

2.7 'First game won by . . .' (in team event, use name of country/team) '. . .' (score)

2.8 'Second game won by . . .' (in team event, use name of country/team) '. . .' (score)

2.9 'Are you setting?'

    2.9.1 'Game not set; playing to 15 (11) points'

    2.9.2 'Setting to 17 (13) points'

2.10 'Court . . .' (number) 'a 90 second interval has been claimed'

2.11 'Court . . .' (number) '20 seconds remaining'

2.12 'One game all'

2.13 'Court . . .' (number) 'a five minute interval has been claimed'

2.14 'Court . . .' (number) 'two minutes remaining'

2.15 'Court . . .' (number) 'one minute remaining'

3. GENERAL COMMUNICATION

3.1 'Are you ready?'

3.2 'Come here'

3.3 'Is the shuttle OK?'

3.4 'Test the shuttle'

3.5 'Change the shuttle'

3.6 'Do not change the shuttle'

3.7 'Play a let'

3.8 'Change ends'

3.9 'You served out of turn'

3.10 'You received out of turn'

3.11 'You must not interfere with the shuttle'

3.12 'The shuttle touched you'
3.13 'You touched the net'
3.14 'You are standing in the wrong court'
3.15 'You distracted your opponent'
3.16 'You hit the shuttle twice'
3.17 'You slung the shuttle'
3.18 'You invaded your opponent's court'
3.19 'You obstructed your opponent'
3.20 'Are you retiring?'
3.21 'Fault–receiver'
3.22 'Service fault called'
3.23 'Play must be continuous'
3.24 'Play is suspended'
3.25 '. . .' (name of player) 'warning for misconduct'
3.26 '. . .' (name of player) 'fault for misconduct'
3.27 'Fault'
3.28 'Out'
3.29 'Line judge—signal'
3.30 'Service judge—signal'
3.31 'First server'
3.32 'Second server'
3.33 'Wipe the court'

4. END OF MATCH

4.1 'Match won by . . .' (name of player team) '. . .' (scores)
4.2 '. . .' (name of player/team) 'retired'
4.3 '. . .' (name of player/team) 'disqualified'

5. SCORING

0—Love	6—Six	12—Twelve
1—One	7—Seven	13—Thirteen
2—Two	8—Eight	14—Fourteen
3—Three	9—Nine	15—Fifteen
4—Four	10—Ten	16—Sixteen
5—Five	11—Eleven	17—Seventeen

Appendix B

IBAD CLASSIFICATIONS

SITTING BADMINTON

All athletes with the minimal required disability shall be eligible for sitting badminton.

WHEELCHAIR CLASS 1—DISABILITY OF TRUNK FUNCTION

Trunk function is characterised by no forceful extension from forwards, side-wards and back

- spinal cord lesion with motor loss complete at L4 included
- double above knee amputation till at one third from the hip.

WHEELCHAIR CLASS 2—NON DISABILITIES OF TRUNK FUNCTIONS

All athletes with a minimal disability as mentioned above (from the hip) are eligible

- single above knee amputation
- double below knee amputation
- double above knee longer stump than one third from the hip

STANDING CLASS—ABOVE BODY DISABILITY

Non-playing arm

- muscle strength in the elbow or shoulder is not more than grade 3 on MRC scale

- the range of movement in the shoulder is not more than 25% antiflexion
- the range of movement in the elbow is not more than 25% extension from maximal flexion
- in co-ordination as in spastic monoplegia or co-ordination problems in plexus brachial
- any player who has not got a functional hand ie cannot hold a racket in their non-playing hand.

Playing arm
- muscle strength not more than grade 4 on MRC scale in hitting direction (forehand)
- range of movement: loss of 30–50% for antiflexion of shoulder and extension of elbow
- in co-ordination as in spastic monoplegia and athethosis in slight degree

STANDING CLASS—BELOW BODY DISABILITY

At least one leg has a loss in forceful push off during jumping, landing and stepping
- stiff ankle, knee or hips
- range of movements
  - no full extension of knee: 30 degrees loss
  - no full extension of hip: 20 degrees loss
- muscle strength
  - not more than grade 3 on MRC scale in plantair flexors of ankle
  - not more than grade 3 on MRC scale in knee extensors
  - not more than grade 3 on MRC scale in hip extensors

A function loss across both legs must be compatible as written for one leg
- in co-ordination as in hemiplegia, spastic monoplegia and diplegia
- amputation below knee single BK class A4

1. COURT AND COURT EQUIPMENT

1.1 The court shall be a rectangle laid out with lines 40 mm wide as in Diagram A in the Laws of Badminton. The following courts shall be used for the disabled:

   1.1.1 Sitting badminton: the courts for singles and doubles shall be as shown in Diagrams F and G, respectively.

   1.1.2 Wheelchair badminton: the courts for singles and doubles shall be as shown in Diagrams H and I, respectively.

   1.1.3 Standing badminton: the courts for singles and doubles shall be as shown in Diagrams J and K, respectively.

Diagram F

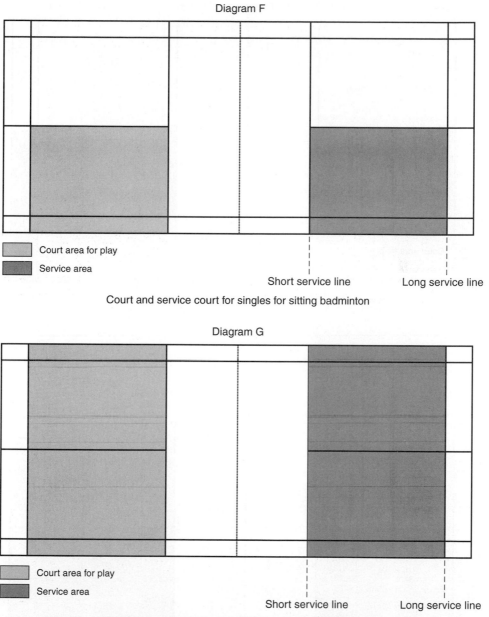

Court area for play

Service area

Short service line   Long service line

Court and service court for singles for sitting badminton

Diagram G

Court area for play

Service area

Short service line   Long service line

Court and service court for doubles for sitting badminton

1.4   The posts shall be the following heights from the surface of the court and shall remain vertical when the net is strained as provided in Law 1.10:

1.4.1 Sitting badminton: 1.20 metres.
1.4.2 Wheelchair badminton: 1.40 metres.
1.4.3 Standing badminton: 1.55 metres.

Diagram H

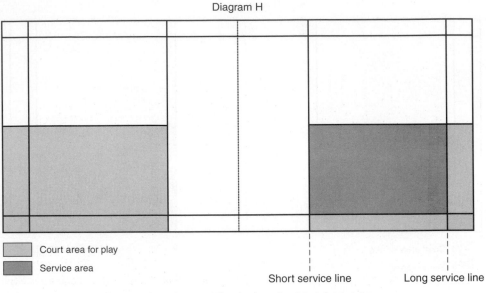

Court area for play

Service area

Short service line   Long service line

Court and service court for singles wheelchair badminton

Diagram I

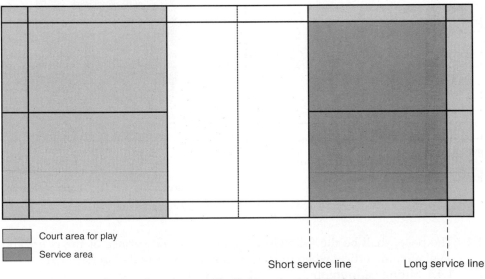

Court area for play

Service area

Short service line   Long service line

Court and service court for doubles wheelchair badminton

Diagram J

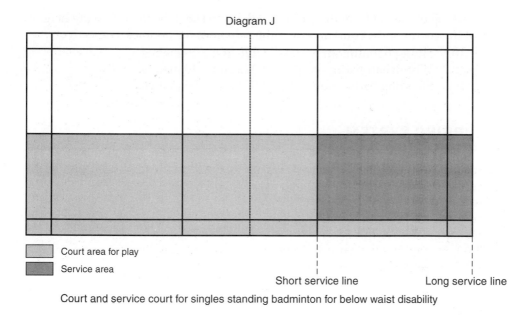

Court area for play

Service area

Short service line   Long service line

Court and service court for singles standing badminton for below waist disability

Diagram K

Court area for play

Service area

Short service line   Long service line

Court and service court for doubles standing badminton for below waist disability

Above body disability courts

Above body disability will play normal court size in accordance with IBF Laws for both singles and doubles

1.10 The top of the net from the surface of the court shall be the following heights at the centre of the court and over the side lines for doubles, respectively:

    1.10.1 Sitting badminton: 1.176 and 1.20 metres.
    1.10.2 Wheelchair badminton: 1.372 and 1.40 metres.
    1.10.3 Standing badminton: 1.524 and 1.55 metres.

7. SCORING SYSTEM

7.2 In all singles and doubles, a game is won by the first side to score 15 points, except as provided in Law 7.4.

7.3 (delete).

7.4 If the score becomes 14-all, the side which first scored 14 shall exercise the choice in Law 7.4.1 or 7.4.2.

    7.4.1 to continue the game to 15 points, i.e., not to 'set' the game; or
    7.4.2 to 'set' the game to 17 points.

8. CHANGE OF ENDS

8.1.3 (delete "- 6 in a game of 11 points; or")

9. SERVICE

9.1 In a correct service:

    9.1.2 the server and receiver shall stand within diagonally opposite service courts or be within the respective service courts without touching the boundary lines of these service courts;

    9 1.3 in standing badminton, upper body disability, the player can only serve and play with one hand, some part of both feet of the server and receiver shall remain in contact with the surface of the court in a stationary position from the start of the service (law 9.4) until the service is delivered; in standing badminton, below body disability, the player shall serve and receive service as provided in Law 9.1.3 with the exception that the player shall have only one foot in contact with the surface of the court;

    9.1.5 in standing badminton the whole shuttle shall be below the server's waist at the instant of being hit by the server's racket; in sitting and wheelchair badminton, the whole shuttle shall be below the server's armpit at the instant of being hit by the server's racket:

    9.1.6 (applies to standing badminton only).

    9.1.9 in wheelchair service no forceful movement is allowed by receiver or server, but slight movement by the server caused by momentum is allowed.

9.7 In doubles for standing badminton the partners may take up any positions which do not unsight the opposing server or receiver and in doubles for sitting and wheelchair badminton, the partners shall be in the adjoining service court.

10. SINGLES

10.1 *Serving and receiving courts*
    10.1.1 The players shall serve from, and receive in, their respective service courts.
    10.1.2 (delete).
10.3 *Scoring and serving*
    10.3.1 (delete "from the alternate service court").

11. DOUBLES

11.5 *Serving and receiving courts*
    11.5.1 In standing badminton, the player who serves (or receives) at the start of any game shall serve from (or receive in) the right service court when that player's side has not scored or has scored an even number of points in that game, and the left service court when that player's side has scored an odd number of points in that game. In sitting badminton the player who serves or receives the service at the start of any game shall serve and receive in the right service court during the game.
    11.5.2 In standing badminton, the reverse pattern shall apply to the partners. In sitting badminton, the partner shall serve and receive in the left service court during the game.
    11.5.3 In standing badminton only, the server shall serve to the diagonally opposite service court when that player's side has not scored or has scored an even number of points.
    11.5.4 In sitting badminton only, the server shall serve to the straight opposite service court when that player's side has scored an odd number of points.

18. LIMITATION OF MOVEMENT

18.1 In wheelchair badminton, at the moment a player strikes the shuttle some part of the trunk shall be in contact with the seat of the wheelchair, both feet or foot shall be on the footplate of the chair at all times, legs should be strapped together unless recommended by the medical officer otherwise.
18.2 In sitting badminton, at the moment that a player strikes the shuttle some part of the trunk shall be in contact with the floor.

Appendix C

The Laws express all measurements in metres or millimetres. Imperial measurements are acceptable and for the purposes of the Laws the following table of equivalence should be used:

Millimetres	Inches
15	⅝
20	¾
25	1
28	1 ⅛
40	1 ½
58	2 ¼
64	2 ½
68	2 ⅝
70	2 ¾
75	3
220	8 ⅝
230	9
280	11
290	11 ⅜

Millimetres	Feet	Inches
380	1	3
420	1	4 ½
490	1	7 ½
530	1	9
570	1	10 ½
680	2	2 ¾
720	2	4 ½
760	2	6
950	3	1 ½
990	3	3

Metres	Feet	Inches
1.524	5	
1.550	5	1
2.530	8	3 ¾
3.880	12	9
4.640	15	3
5.180	17	
6.100	20	
13.400	44	

GLOSSARY

Every modern sport has its own particular terminology, and badminton is no exception. Often, these terms seem peculiar to the beginner, but they arise from fascinating origins. Pursuing the origins of the language of individual sports would provide many hours of interesting research.

For example, what explains the "side" of badminton's terms "side-in" and "side-out"? A bit of investigation reveals that in its early years the game was played by sides consisting of at least three players, and usually four or five. Singles and doubles were nonexistent. Instead, a team consisted of several players who served in turn until they were individually eliminated. When all team members had finished serving, thus completing an "inning," that group was said to be "side-out." Currently, the term "service-over" is used in the laws, but players continue to say "side-out."

The derivations of the terms presented in the following glossary are equally fascinating, and pursuit of them by the curious student would promise interesting results. Some of them have been more fully described in the chapters of this book.

A

ALLEY Extension of the court by one-and-one-half feet on both sides for doubles play.

ANTICIPATION The art of foreseeing an opponent's next shot.

B

BACK ALLEY Area between the back boundary line and the long service line for doubles.

BACKCOURT The back third of the court, in the area of the back boundary lines.

BACKHAND Refers to strokes played on the nonracket side of the body (*i.e.*, with the racket across the body).

BACKSWING Preliminary part of a stroke that carries the racket back in preparation for the forward swing.

BALK Any deceptive movement that disconcerts an opponent before or during the service; often called a "feint."

BASELINE Back boundary line at each end of the court, parallel to the net.

BIRD The informal name for badminton's unique object, the shuttlecock; brand names include Bluebird, Eagle, and Parrot.

BLOCK A stationary stroke, executed by holding the racket in the path of a smashed shuttle, so that it rebounds into the opponent's court.

C

CARRY An illegal tactic, also called sling or throw, in which the shuttle is caught and held on the racket and then slung during the execution of a stroke.

CENTER OR BASE POSITION Location in the center of the court to which a singles player tries to return after each shot.

CENTER LINE Line perpendicular to the net that separates the left and right service courts.

CLEAR A shot hit deep to the opponent's back boundary line. The *high clear* is a defensive shot, while the flatter *attacking clear* is used offensively.

COURT Area of play, as defined by the outer boundary lines.

CROSSCOURT A shot hit diagonally from one side of the court to the other.

D

DECEPTION The art of deceiving one's opponent by outright feinting or by disguising a shot's direction and speed until the last moment.

DEFENSE State of being under attack by the opponent; a style of play consisting mainly of slow drops and high clears.

DOUBLE HIT An illegal tactic in which the shuttle is hit twice in succession with two strokes.

DOUBLES The game played with two players on each side.

DRIVE A fast and low shot that makes a horizontal flight over the net.

DRIVE SERVE A hard, quick serve with a flat trajectory, often used to upset an opponent's pace.

DROP A shot hit softly and with finesse to fall rapidly and close to the net on the opponent's side.

E

ENDS (OF COURT) The sections of court on either side of the net, as in "changing ends."

F

FACE The oval, stringed area of the racket head.

FAULT A violation of the playing rules, either in serving, in receiving, or during play. See Law 14.

FIRST SERVER In doubles, the player who serves first for a side during a particular inning.

FLAT Describes the flight of a shuttle with a horizontal trajectory and the angle of the racket face when hitting the shuttle with no "slicing" action.

FLICK A quick wrist and forearm rotation that surprises an opponent by changing an apparently soft shot into a faster passing one; used primarily on the serve and at the net.

FLIGHT The path or trajectory of the shuttle.

FOLLOW-THROUGH That part of a stroke coming after the racket's impact with the shuttle.

FOOT FAULT A violation of the rules in which the feet of the server or receiver are not in the position required by the laws.

FOOTWORK The patterns of foot movement in moving about the court.

FORECOURT The front third of the court; between the net and the short service line.

FOREHAND Refers to strokes played on the racket side of the body.

FORWARD SWING That part of a stroke carrying the racket forward to the point of contact with the shuttle.

G

GAME A unit of points necessary for victory: a game consists of fifteen points in men's singles and in all doubles, while eleven points constitutes a game in women's singles. See also "Setting."

GAME POINT A rally which, if won by the server, ends the game. Also called "game bird."

GRIP The hold on the racket.

H

HAIRPIN DROP A shot made from below and close to the net with the shuttle rising, just clearing the net, and then dropping sharply down the other side. The shuttle's flight approximates the shape of a hairpin.

HALF-COURT SHOT A shot hit low and to midcourt, used effectively in doubles against the up-and-back formation.

HAND An outdated term meaning server, as in "first hand" for "first server."

HEAD The end of the racket used for hitting the shuttle (*i.e.*, the strings and the surrounding oval frame).

I

IBF International Badminton Federation, the world governing body established in 1934.

INNING Time during which a player or team holds the service.

IN PLAY The shuttle is "in play" from the time it is struck by the server's racket until it touches the court or a fault or let occurs.

"IN" SIDE The side that holds the serve.

K

KILL A fast, downward shot that cannot be returned; a "putaway."

L

LET A legitimate cessation of play to allow a rally to be replayed.

LONG SERVICE LINE In singles, the back boundary line; in doubles, a line two-and-one-half feet inside the back boundary line. The serve may not go past this line.

LOVE Term for zero arising from the English pronunciation of the French word *l'oeuf*, meaning "goose-egg" or zero.

LOVE-ALL No score (*i.e.*, zero to zero). To start a match, the umpire calls, "Love-All, Play."

M

MATCH A series of games, usually two out of three, to determine a winner.

MATCH POINT A rally that, if won by the server, ends the match.

MIDCOURT The middle third of the court; halfway between the net and the back boundary line.

N

NET SHOT Shot hit from the forecourt that just clears the net and drops sharply.

NO SHOT Call made by a player who faults by committing a carry or double hit. Badminton sportsmanship requires that, in the absence of an umpire, players make such calls on themselves.

O

OBSTRUCTION An illegal tactic in which a player hinders an opponent in the making of a shot.

OFFENSE State of being on the attack; a style of play consisting mainly of attacking clears, fast drops, and smashes.

OUT Call made by a line judge or player when the shuttle lands outside the boundary lines.

"OUT" SIDE The side receiving the serve.

OVERHEAD Refers to stroke played above head level.

P

POINT Smallest unit in scoring.

POONA Early name for badminton in India, coming from a city in which a badminton-like game was played from the 1860s.

PRONATION The inward turning of the wrist and forearm used in all powerful overhead forehand strokes.

PUSH SHOT A gentle shot played by pushing the shuttle with little wrist motion, usually from net or midcourt to the opponent's midcourt.

R

RACKET The implement used to hit the shuttle.

RALLY An exchange of shots while the shuttle is in play.

READY POSITION An alert body position enabling the player to make quick movement in any direction.

RECEIVER The player to whom the service is delivered.

ROTATION Rotation of the side-by-side and up-and-back doubles formations.

ROUND-THE-HEAD STROKE An overhead forehand stroke played on the backhand side of the body. The contact point is usually above the opposite shoulder, and a clear, drop, or smash can result.

RUSH THE SERVE Quick move to the net in an attempt to put away a low serve by smashing or driving the shuttle out of reach. Used mostly in doubles.

S

SECOND SERVER In doubles, the partner who has second turn at serving for a side during a particular inning.

SERVE OR SERVICE Stroke used to put the shuttle into play at the start of each rally.

SERVICE COURT Area into which the serve must be delivered. This depends on the score and on whether the game is singles or doubles.

SETTING Method of extending a tied game by increasing the number of points necessary to win. Player reaching the tied score first has option of setting.

SETUP A poor shot that makes an easy kill for the opponent.

SHAFT The part of the racket between the head and the handle.

SHORT SERVICE LINE The line six-and-one-half feet from the net that a serve must reach to be legal.

SHOT The result of a stroke; a shot will be good or bad depending on the execution of the stroke.

SHUTTLECOCK Official (and ancient) name for shuttle or "bird," badminton's unique projectile.

SIDEARM Refers to a stroke played with the arm out to the side of the body.

SIDE-BY-SIDE A doubles formation.

SIDE-IN AND SIDE-OUT See text at the beginning of the glossary.

SMASH A hard-hit overhead shot that forces the shuttle sharply downward. It is badminton's chief attacking stroke.

STROKE Action of striking the shuttle with the racket.

SUPINATION The outward turning of the wrist and forearm used on all powerful backhand strokes.

T

THROAT That part of the racket where the shaft joins the head.

TOSS Before play begins, opponents must toss a coin or spin a racket. The winner may elect to serve, to receive, or to choose an end; the loser has any choice remaining.

U

USA BADMINTON The national governing body for badminton in the United States, founded in 1936 as the American Badminton Association and known from 1978 to 1998 as the United States Badminton Association.

UNDERHAND Refers to a stroke that contacts the shuttle below the waist, such as a serve or a clear from the net.

UNSIGHT In doubles, to stand in such a way that an opponent cannot see the serve being delivered. This is an obstruction and is illegal.

UP-AND-BACK A doubles formation, particularly predominant in mixed doubles.

W

WOOD SHOT A shot that results when the base of the shuttle is hit by the frame of the racket. Once illegal, this shot was ruled acceptable by the IBF in 1963.

REFERENCES

GENERAL BOOKS ABOUT BADMINTON

Adams, B. 1980. *The Badminton Story*. London: British Broadcasting Publications.

Davis, P. 1983. *The Guinness Book of Badminton*. London: Guinness Superlatives Ltd. (Order from Sterling).

Hales, D. 1979. A History of Badminton in the United States from 1878–1939. Master's thesis, California State Polytechnic University.

BOOKS FOR PLAYERS AND COACHES

Many are now out of print but often available in libraries; those known still to be in print are marked with an asterisk—*.

Aberdare, C. 1933. *Rackets, Squash Rackets, Tennis, Fives, and Badminton*. Philadelphia: J. B. Lippincott.

Annarino, A. A. 1973. *Badminton: Individualized Instructional Program*. Englewood Cliffs, NJ: Prentice-Hall.

*Badminton Association of England, ed. 1994. *Know the Game—Badminton*. London: Black.

Ballou, R. B. 1982. *Teaching Badminton* (Sport Teaching Series). New York: Burgess.

———. 1992. *Badminton for Beginners*. Englewood, CO: Morton Publishing Co.

*Boga, S. 1996. *Badminton*. Mechanicsburg, PA: Stackpole Books.

Breen, J. L. 1969. *Badminton*. Chicago: Athletic Institute.

*Breen, J. L., and D. Paup. 1983. *Winning Badminton: A Coaching and Playing Guide*. North Palm Beach: Athletic Institute.

Brown, E. *The Complete Book of Badminton*. Harrisburg, PA: Stackpole Books.

*Boy Scouts of America. 1986. *Cub Scout Sports: Badminton*.

Burris, B., and A. Olson. 1970. *Badminton* (Sports Techniques Series). Chicago: Athletic Institute.

————. 1974. *Badminton*. Boston: Allyn and Bacon.

*Chafin, M. B., and M. M. Turner. 1988. *Badminton Everyone*. Winston-Salem, NC: Hunter Textbooks.

Choong, E., and F. Brundle. 1953. *Badminton*. New York: Dover Publications.

————. 1956. *The Phoenix Book of Badminton*. London: Phoenix House.

Crossley, K. G. *Progressive Badminton*. New Rochelle (NY): Sportshelf, 1979; London: Bell Publishers, rev. 1980.

Davidson, K. R., and L. R. Gustavson. *Winning Badminton*. New York: A. S. Barnes and Company, 1953; New York: Ronald Press Co., 1964; Melbourne (FL): Krieger Publishing Co., rev. 1964.

Davidson, K. R., and L. C. Smith. 1961. *Badminton* (Athletic Institute Series). New York: Sterling Publishing Co., Inc.

Davis, P. 1980. *The Badminton Coach: A Manual for Coaches, Teachers, and Players*. New Rochelle, NY: Sportshelf.

————. *Badminton Complete*. London: Kaye and Ward, 1967, rev. 1982; South Brunswick (NJ): A. S. Barnes, 1976.

————. 1988. *Badminton*. London: Ward Lock.

————. *Badminton, A Complete Practical Guide*. London: David and Charles, 1989; London: Blandford, 1993.

Devlin, J. F. 1937. *Badminton for All*. Garden City, NY: Doubleday, Doran and Company, Inc.

Devlin, J. F., and R. Lardner. *Sports Illustrated Book of Badminton*. Philadelphia: Lippincott, 1967. Harcourt-Row, 1973.

Dick, T. P. 1939. *Badminton*. London: G. Bell & Sons.

Downey, J. C. 1975. *Better Badminton for All*. London: Kaye and Ward.

————. 1978. *Badminton for Schools*. London: Pelham Books.

————. 1983. *Winning Badminton Singles*. London: E. P. Publishing Co.

————. 1984. *Winning Badminton Doubles*. London: Adam and Charles Black.

————. 1994. *Excelling at Badminton*. Trafalgar Square: Hodst.

*Dugas, E. 1989. *Badminton Made Simple*. New York: McGraw-Hill Companies. E. Bowers.

Edgren, H. D. 1939. *Group Instruction in Tennis and Badminton*. New York: A. S. Barnes.

Fahrman, L. 1987. *Badminton Bonanza*. Durham: Great Activities Publishing Co.

Finston, I., and C. Remsberg. 1979. *Inside Badminton*. Chicago: Contemporary Books, Inc.

Fisher, H. 1939. *How to Play Badminton*. Minneapolis: Burgess.

Fitz Gibbon, H. S., II, and J. N. Bairstow. 1979. *The Complete Racquet Sports Player*. New York: Simon & Schuster.

Friedrich, J., and A. Rutledge. *Beginning Badminton*. Belmont (CA): Wadsworth Publishing Co., Inc., 1962; rev. 1969.

Grant, D. 1950. *Badminton: The International Textbook of the Game*. Montreal: Graphics Publishing Co.

*Grice, W. A. 1981. *Badminton*. Boston: American Press.

*————. 1996. *Badminton: Steps to Success*. Champaign, IL: Human Kinetics.

Hashman, J. D., 1969. *A Champion's Way*. London: Kaye and Ward.

————. 1984. *Winning Badminton*. London: Ward Lock.

Hashman, J. D., and C. M. Jones. 1977. *Beginning Badminton*. New York: Arco Publishing.

Hicks, V. 1973. *The How to of Badminton From Player to Teacher*. Denton, TX: Terrell Wheeler Printing, Inc.

Jackson, C. H., and L. A. Swan. 1938. *Badminton Tips*. Detroit: Sports Tips and Teaching Aids.

————. 1939. *Better Badminton*. New York: A. S. Barnes & Company.

Johnson, M. L. 1974. *Badminton*. Philadelphia: W. B. Saunders Co.

*Johnson, M. L., and D. Johnson. 1981. *Badminton*. Boston: American Press.

*Krotee, M. L., and E. Turner. 1984. *Innovative Theory and Practice of Badminton*. Dubuque, IA: Kendall-Hunt.

Larminie, M. R. 1926. *Badminton for Beginners*. London: Chatto & Windus.

*Mills, R. J. 1975. *Badminton*. London: E. P. Publishing, Ltd.

Mills, R. J., and E. Butler. 1974. *Tackle Badminton*. London: Paul.

Moore, B. J. and T. E. Henderson. 1977. *Shuttlecock Action*. Dubuque, IA: Kendall-Hunt.

Pearson, P. 1985. *Teaching and Coaching Junior Badminton*. Cheshire, England: Cheshire Press.

Pelton, B. C. 1971. *Badminton*. Englewood Cliffs: Prentice-Hall.

*Poole, J. 1996. *Badminton*. 4th ed. Prospect Heights, IL: Waveland Press.

Post, J. 1933. *Selected Recreational Sports for Girls and Women*. New York: A. S. Barnes.

Prior, J. C. *How to Play Badminton*. London: A. G. Spaulding.

Radford, N. 1954. *Badminton*. London: I. Pitman.

Rangecroft, C. 1956. *The Right Way to Play Badminton*. London: Elliot's Books.

*Reznik, J., and R. Byrd. 1987. *Badminton*. Scottsdale, AZ: Gorsuch-Scarisbrick.

*Robertson, K., and D. Abbott. 1989. *GWR: The Badminton Line: a portrait of a railway*. Dover: A. Sutton Publishing.

Rogers, T. W. 1970. *Advanced Badminton* (Physical Education Activities Series). New York: McGraw-Hill Companies.

*Roper, P. 1985. *Badminton: The Skills of the Game*. Marlborough, England: Crowood Press.

Squires, D. 1978. *The Other Racket Sports*. Chap. 6. New York: McGraw-Hill Companies.

*Stevenson, S. 1980. *Badminton Handbook*. N. Vancouver: Hancock House.

Sullivan, G. 1968. *Guide to Badminton*. New York: Fleet Press Corp.

*Sweeting, R. L. 1992. *Badminton: Basic Skills and Drills*. Mountain View, CA: Mayfield Publishing Co.

Talbot, D. 1981. *Badminton to the Top*. Wakefield, England: E. P. Publishing Limited.

Thomas, Sir George. 1923. *The Art of Badminton*. London: Hutchinson.

Uber, E. 1936. *Badminton*. London: Eyre & Spottiswoode.

Watson, A. 1976. *Winning Badminton*. Toronto: Coles Publishing Co.

Whetnall, P., and T. Leahy. 1987. *Badminton* (Competitive Sports Services). London: Batsford.

Wright, L. 1972. *Your Book of Badminton*. London: Faber and Faber Publishers.

———. 1982. *Successful Badminton*. London: Letts & Co. Ltd.

TEACHING AND COACHING GUIDES

A Basic Guide to Badminton. United States Olympic Committee. 1988. Glendale, CA: Griffin Publishing.

Badminton-Squash-Racquetball Guide. NAGWS-AAHPER, 1900 Association Drive, Reston, VA, 22091-9989. (Once known as *Tennis, Badminton, and Squash Guide*.)

First Coaching Seminar, Peking, China, March 26–April 2, 1977. Asian Badminton Confederation, c/o Karen Koh, WTC Club, Country Heights, 43000 Kajang, Selangor Darul Ehsan, Kuala Lumpur, Malaysia.

National Coaching Certification Manuals, Levels 1–3. Badminton Canada, 1600 James Naismith Drive, Gloucester, Ontario, K1B 5N4, Canada.

Selected Tennis and Badminton Articles. NAGWS-AAHPER, 1900 Association Drive, Reston, VA, 23091-9989.

PHOTOGRAPH BOOKS AND CDS

Ross, L. 1982. *Badminton Picture Book: Masters 80*. Southampton, England: Louis Ross Books.

———. 1984. *Badminton in Europe*. Southampton, England: Louis Ross Books.

———. 1984. *Hundred Plus Badminton Players*. Southampton, England: Louis Ross Books.

———. 1998. *1998 All England Championships*. Louis Ross Photography. (Photos on CD).

[84 Rumbridge St., Totton, Southampton SO4 4DS, England].

RULES BOOKS

Badminton Canada Handbook (Rule Book). Badminton Canada, 1600 James Naismith Drive, Gloucester, Ontario, K1B 5N4, Canada.

I. B. F. Statute Book. The International Badminton Federation, Manor Park Place, Rutherford Way, Cheltenham, Gloucestershire, GL51 9TU, UK.

Official Rules of Play (USAB Handbook). USA Badminton, 1 Olympic Plaza, Colorado Springs, CO, 80909.

MAGAZINES

Asian Badminton. Asian Badminton Confederation, c/o Karen Koh, WTC Club, Country Heights, 43000 Kajang, Selangor Darul Ehsan, Kuala Lumpur, Malaysia.

Badminton Canada Bulletin. Badminton Canada, 1600 James Naismith Drive, Gloucester, Ontario, K1B 5N4, Canada.

Badminton Now. The Badminton Association of England, National Badminton Centre, Bradwell Road, Loughton Lodge, Milton Keynes MK8 9LA, England.

Badminton U.S.A. USA Badminton, 1 Olympic Plaza, Colorado Springs, CO, 80909.

China Sports. China Books and Periodicals, 2929 24th Street, San Francisco, CA, 94110.

World Badminton. The International Badminton Federation, Manor Park Place, Rutherford Way, Cheltenham, Gloucestershire, GL51 9TU, UK. [on-line publication at http://www.worldbadminton.org.]

FILMS AND VIDEOS

Badminton Movies. Louisville Badminton Supply, 9411 Westport Road, Louisville, KY, 40222.

Badminton Sound Films. AAHPERD Educational Media Services, 1201 16th Street NW, Washington DC, 20036.

Badminton Sound Super 8 Cassettes. 1974. AAHPERD Educational Media Services, 1201 16th Street NW, Washington DC, 20036.

Badminton—Winning Fundamentals. Cambridge P. E. and Health.

C. B. A. Video Library. Badminton Canada, 1600 James Naismith Drive, Gloucester, Ontario, K1B 5N4, Canada.

Selected Highlights of the 1973 U.S. Open Amateur Championships. Travelers Insurance Companies, 1 Tower Square, Hartford, CT, 06115.

U. S. A. B. Video Library (videocassettes of national and international events). USA Badminton, 1 Olympic Plaza, Colorado Springs, CO, 80909.

INDEX

147